INTRODUCTION

▲▲▲▲▲▲▲▲▲▲▲▲▲▲▲

Maths Maintenance 4 is one in a series of student activity books designed to complement the N.S.W. Mathematics K-6 Syllabus and the Resource Materials for Basic Learning K-6 Mathematics.

This series is designed to consolidate and maintain known concepts and to present new mathematical concepts in an interesting and fun way. Students are encouraged to explore their mathematical environment through a mixture of practical hands-on activities and pen and paper activities. A scope and sequence chart is included which also links the material in the book to the N.S.W. Mathematics K-6 Syllabus.

This activity book can be used in the classroom, for homework, or both. Parents are encouraged to be involved and a four-page pull-out answer section is provided to assist them.

There are 30 units in the activity book. Each unit covers the mathematical areas of Number, Measurement and Space. In each Number  section there is a speed drill, marked with a clockface which allows for practice in instant written recall of number facts.

Every fifth unit is a theme unit which integrates Number, Measurement and Space.

At the end of each unit students are encouraged to assess and evaluate their own progress by writing about their work on page 64. The teacher, parent or student can also initial or colour the boxes to indicate work completed.

SCOPE AND SEQUENCE YEAR 4

▲▲▲▲▲▲▲▲▲▲▲▲▲▲▲▲▲▲▲▲

UNIT	NUMBER		SPEED	MEASUREMENT		SPACE	
1	2-digit plus 1-digit 3-digit numbers – ordering Value off digit	A6 N12 N12	x 2, 4, 1	**Length** – measuring in centimetres	L10	**3D** – constructing a net	3D9
2	2 minus 1 digit 3 times Division – sharing	S9 M6 D5	x 10, 50	**Area** – using informal units	A6	**Position** – sketching a route. Instructions for a pattern	P4
3	3 times Adding – 2-digit algorithms Matching decimals	M6 A6 F&D7	+, – Combinations to 20	**Time** – matching an activity to time	T12	**Graphs** – interpreting tally marks and column graphs	G3
4	3 times and 6 times Reading prices Subtraction – 2 place algorithm	M6 Mon4 CM	2 digit + 1 digit	**Mass** – comparing objects to 1 kg mass	M10	**2D** – lines of symmetry	2D13
5	**Theme – The Zoo**						
6	6 times Introducing 1 000 – concrete materials Division 6	M6 N13	3 times 2 digit – 1 digit	**Volume** – comparing capacity to 1 litre. Measuring larger containers	V11	**3D** – investigating cross-sections of prisms	3D9
7	9 times 6 times 1000 – concrete materials Division	M6 M6 N13 D6	3 times Adding 2	**Temperature** – comparing temperature – informal using thermometer	T5	**3D** – labelling pyramids	3D10
8	9 times Concepts tenths/hundredths Addition – 2 digit	M6 FD8 A7	6 times Adding 4	**Area** – making a square metre Finding areas smaller and larger	A7	**Position** – marking routes on a map	P4
9	Subtraction 9 times Tenths/hundredths	S10 M6 FD8	6 times Adding 3	**Length** – using metres and centimetres	L10	**2D** – comparing angles	2D14
10	**Theme – Fairytales**						
11	1 000 – reading and writing Relate division and multiplication	N13 D7	9 times Subtracting 2	**Time** – using a school timetable	T13	**2D** – tessellating shapes	2D15
12	1 000 recognise value of digit Rounding off Division and multiplication	N13 D7	9 times Subtracting 4	**Mass** – using half kg masses	M10	**3D** – matching shapes and nets	3D10
13	1 000 ordering Money Calculator	N13 Mon4 N13	3 times and 6 times Subtracting 9	**Area** – using square metre to measure floor areas	A7	**Position** – following simple	P4
14	Before and after 1 000s Fractions and decimals – tenths 8 times	N13 FD9 M7	6 times and 9 times Adding 5	**Length** – writing heights in decimal format	L11	**2D** – tessellations Making a tiling pattern	2D15
15	**Theme – The Circus**						

UNIT	NUMBER		SPEED	MEASUREMENT		SPACE	
16	8 times Fractions and decimals 2-digit addition	M7 FD9 A7	Times and dividing 2, 4 Subtracting 5	**Time** – interpreting a railroad timetable	T13	**2D** – flipping, sliding and turning to make patterns	2D15
17	7 times Division and multiplication 6 2-digit subtraction	M7 S10	Times and dividing 5, 10 Adding 3, 4, 5	**Mass** – identify and classify packages in grams and kilograms	M11	**Graphs** – reading and making a column graph	G
18	7 times Multiplication and division 9 Decimals and fractions	 FD10	Times and dividing 3 Subtracting 3, 4, 5	**Volume** – measuring volume by displacement Measuring to nearest 100 mL	V12	**3D** – recognising solids from top view and side view	3D
19	Multiplication and division 6 and 9 Decimals and fractions Value of notes	M6 FD10 Mon5	Times 8 Adding 6, 7	**Length** – measuring circumference using string or by rolling	L11	**Position** – drawing a plan and writing directions	P
20	**Theme – At the Shopping Centre**						
21	Factors 1 000s – place value Calculator	M8 N13 FD10	Times 8 Subtracting 6, 7	**Area** – measuring in square centimetres	A8	**2D** – reassembling shapes	2D
22	Multiples Money – notes, coins, value	M8 Mon5	Times 7 Adding 8, 9	**Time** – using a.m. and p.m.	T13	**3D** – different perspectives of solids	3D
23	Multiplication number stories Addition algorithms 1 000s – trading and rounding off	M8 A7 N13	Times 7 Subtracting 8, 9	**Length** – comparing lengths written in decimal form (to tenths)	L11	**Position** – making a maze	P
24	Code Fractions and decimals Subtraction, algorithm, tradings	 FD10 S11	Times and dividing 6 Adding 6, 7, 8, 9	**Mass** – comparing standard mass pieces to 1 kg	M11	**3D** – various views of solids	3D
25	**Theme – Pirates**						
26	Factors and multiplies Tracks 1 000s	M8 D9 N13	Dividing and times 9 Subtracting 6, 7, 8, 9	**Volume** – comparing volumes in mL	V12	**2D** – tangrams	2D
27	Division stories Value – 1 000s – adding to Crossnumber puzzle	D10 N13	Division and times 7 Mixed multiplication	**Temperature** – using informal scales with thermometer	T6	**2D** – paper folding to make shapes	2D
28	Money – change Fractions and decimals Division remainder	Mon5 FD10 D10	Dividing and times 7 Mixed multiplication	**Area** – measuring in cm^2 shapes on grid paper	A8	**Position** – investigate placement	P
29	Tracks	D9	Mixed multiplication	**Time** – recall time facts	T14	**2D** – transformations with geostrips	2D
30	**Theme – Let's Go On A Vacation**						

UNIT 1
▲▲▲▲▲

NUMBER

Add these and write each answer in the box beside.

1.  + ▦▦ = | 578 |

2. ▦ + ▦▦ = | 68 |

3. ▦ + ▦▦ = | 89 |

4. ▦ + ▦▦ = | 68 |

What place values have the following numbers?

1. | 368 | 6 tens

2. | 155 | 1 hundred

3. | 973 | 3 ones

4. | 406 | 4 hundreds

1. 2 x 2 = 4	1. 2 x 9 = 18
2. 4 x 5 = 20	2. 4 x 1 = 4
3. 2 x 4 = 8	3. 7 x 1 = 7
4. 4 x 8 = 32	4. 2 x 8 = 16
5. 2 x 5 = 10	5. 2 x 10 = 20
6. 5 x 1 = 5	6. 4 x 8 = 32
7. 2 x 8 = 16	7. 8 x 1 = 8
8. 4 x 3 = 12	8. 4 x 2 = 8
9. 2 x 1 = 2	9. 2 x 7 = 14
10. 4 x 9 = 36	10. 3 x 4 = 12
11. 7 x 1 = 7	11. 2 x 6 = 12
12. 4 x 6 = 24	12. 4 x 7 = 28
13. 2 x 7 = 14	13. 4 x 4 = 16
14. 4 x 4 = 16	14. 9 x 4 = 36
15. 2 x 6 = 12	15. 2 x 5 = 10
16. 2 x 0 = 0	16. 4 x 0 = 0
17. 4 x 10 = 40	17. 4 x 5 = 20
18. 8 x 1 = 8	18. 6 x 1 = 6
19. 4 x 7 = 28	19. 4 x 2 = 8
20. 6 x 1 = 6	20. 4 x 6 = 24

▲▲

MEASUREMENT
Estimate, then measure each path in centimetres.

1. Rosa's path is __14½__ cm long.

2. Sue's path is __16__ cm long.

3. Marcia's path is __17½__ cm long.

4. __Marcia's__ path is longest.

5. __Rosa's__ path is the shortest.

6. How many more cm is Marcia's path than Rosa's? __2.5__

Match each number with a numeral expander by writing the correct number in the box after the numeral expander.

1.	164	2	hundreds	5	tens	3	ones	253
2.	507	9	hundreds	0	tens	9	ones	909
3.	378	6	hundreds	9	tens	0	ones	690
4.	690	1	hundred	6	tens	4	ones	164
5.	253	5	hundreds	0	tens	7	ones	507
6.	909	3	hundreds	7	tens	8	ones	378

Write these numbers in the correct sequence from smallest to largest.

| 302 | 294 | 286 | 278 | 306 | 282 | 290 | 298 |

278, 282, 286, 290, 294, 298, 302, 306.

S P A C E

Find an empty cereal box, food packet or tissue box.

Look at it carefully and then draw what you think its net would be like.

Then take the box apart carefully and see how accurate you were.

Use another colour to correct the net you have drawn – if you need to!

NUMBER

1. Count on in threes.

0 __ __ __ __ __ __ __ __ __

__ __ __ __ __ __ __ __ __ __

2. Now use the numbers you have written to complete these number sentences.

3 x 1 = ☐   3 x 2 = ☐   3 x 3 = ☐   3 x 4 = ☐

3 x 5 = ☐   3 x 6 = ☐   3 x 7 = ☐   3 x 8 = ☐

3 x 9 = ☐   3 x 10 = ☐

3. What is the distance between these towns?

(a) | Leeds 17 km
    | Milton 3 km
    | ☐ km

(b) | Grafton 19 km
    | Tomer 6 km
    | ☐ km

(c) | Grover 15 km
    | Albion 9 km
    | ☐ km

4. What is the difference between the ages below?

(a) | Morris 16
    | Tara 11
    | ☐ years

(b) | Ali 18
    | Karl 9
    | ☐ years

(c) | Yumiko 13
    | Daniel 8
    | ☐ years

1. 10 x 1 = ☐	1. ☐ x 5 = 25
2. 5 x 5 = ☐	2. 6 x ☐ = 0
3. 10 x 6 = ☐	3. 10 x 8 = ☐
4. 5 x 6 = ☐	4. ☐ x 5 = 45
5. 10 x 9 = ☐	5. 0 x 8 = ☐
6. 7 x 5 = ☐	6. 5 x ☐ = 15
7. 8 x 10 = ☐	7. ☐ x 9 = 0
8. 5 x 8 = ☐	8. 5 x 6 = ☐
9. 10 x 5 = ☐	9. 5 x ☐ = 10
10. 0 x 4 = ☐	10. ☐ x 9 = 90
11. 4 x 10 = ☐	11. 7 x ☐ = 0
12. 9 x 5 = ☐	12. 5 x ☐ = 20
13. 10 x 7 = ☐	13. 10 x 7 = ☐
14. 0 x 6 = ☐	14. ☐ x 8 = 40
15. 10 x 3 = ☐	15. 10 x ☐ = 70
16. 8 x 0 = ☐	16. 5 x ☐ = 35
17. 2 x 10 = ☐	17. 7 x 0 = ☐
18. 0 x 9 = ☐	18. ☐ x 10 = 10

MEASUREMENT

1. Area = _____ squares

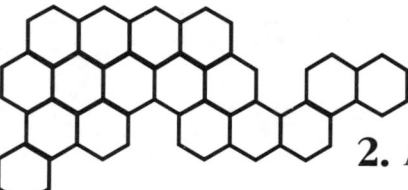

2. Area = _____

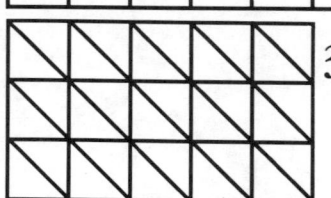

3. Area = _____

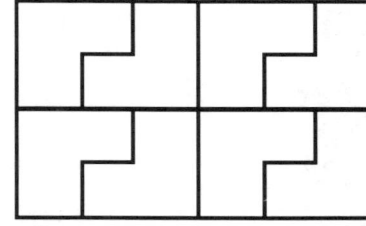

4. Area = _____

Which of these shapes would be good for measuring the area of your desktop?

_____

Why? _____

1. ◺   2. ⌇   3. ⬡

4. ☐   5. ⬭   6. ⌐

You will need Base 10 material or a packet of toothpicks to do these divisions.

Write your answers in the boxes.

1. 54 ÷ 3 = ☐

2. 64 ÷ 4 = ☐

3. 90 ÷ 5 = ☐

4. 72 ÷ 3 = ☐

5. 84 ÷ 6 = ☐

Follow the path and find the answers.

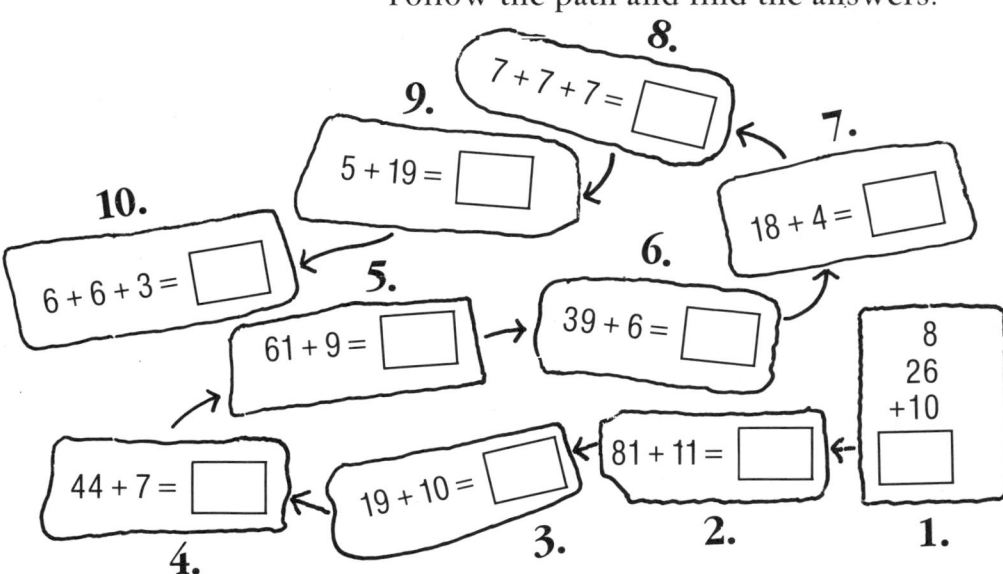

8. 7 + 7 + 7 = ☐

9. 5 + 19 = ☐

10. 6 + 6 + 3 = ☐

7. 18 + 4 = ☐

5. 61 + 9 = ☐

6. 39 + 6 = ☐

1. 8 / 26 / +10 / ☐

2. 81 + 11 = ☐

3. 19 + 10 = ☐

4. 44 + 7 = ☐

▲▲▲

S P A C E

1. Pretend you are a robot. Stand in an open area.

(a) Go forward 4 steps.
(b) Turn right.
(c) Go forward 4 steps.
(d) Turn right.
(e) Go forward 4 steps.
(f) Turn right.
(g) Go forward 4 steps.

What shape have you made on the floor? Draw the shape here.

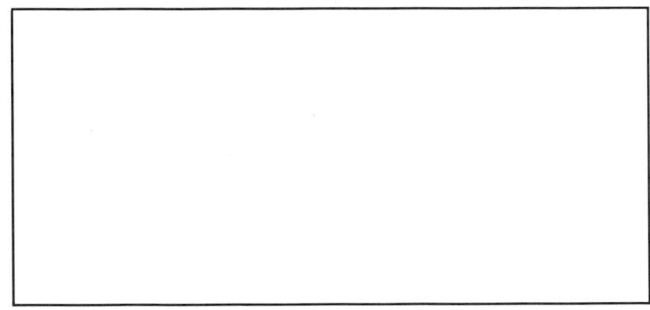

2. Make up another pattern yourself and write instructions for the robot on a piece of paper.

3. What instructions would you give to a robot to create the pattern shown below?

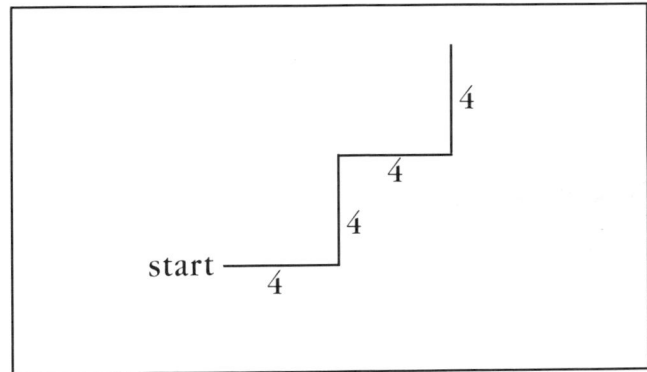

(a) _____

(b) _____

(c) _____

(d) _____

(e) _____

(f) _____

(g) _____

Try the moves with a friend to check if they are correct.

NUMBER

Complete the number pattern by writing in the missing numbers.

+	▯	▯	▯	▯
▯				
▯				
▯				
▯				

1. $14 + \square = 20$ 1. $20 - 10 = \square$
2. $8 + \square = 16$ 2. $17 - 14 = \square$
3. $\square + 17 = 19$ 3. $19 - 8 = \square$
4. $14 + \square = 17$ 4. $20 - 19 = \square$
5. $15 + \square = 20$ 5. $15 - 6 = \square$
6. $\square + 12 = 17$ 6. $20 - 9 = \square$
7. $\square + 6 = 14$ 7. $16 - 6 = \square$
8. $9 + \square = 20$ 8. $18 - 9 = \square$
9. $\square + 15 = 18$ 9. $17 - 3 = \square$
10. $7 + \square = 13$ 10. $20 - 14 = \square$
11. $17 + \square = 20$ 11. $16 - 6 = \square$
12. $\square + 3 = 19$ 12. $20 - 18 = \square$
13. $\square + 9 = 15$ 13. $18 - 8 = \square$
14. $13 + \square = 18$ 14. $20 - 12 = \square$
15. $7 + \square = 16$ 15. $19 - 7 = \square$
16. $\square + 5 = 15$ 16. $13 - 6 = \square$

MEASUREMENT

1. Match the activity to the time. Draw a line from the time to the activity. How long does it take to ...

play a game of football?

boil an egg?

30 minutes

sleep?

2 seconds

8 hours

3 minutes

read a page?

hop twice?

1 hour

write a letter?

5 minutes

2. Put the hands on the clocks.

Almost 9.00

Just after 8.50

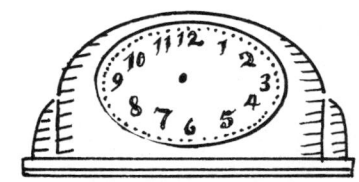
Nearly 2.30

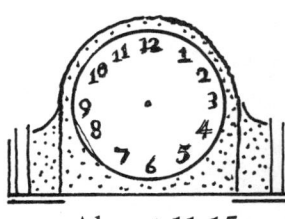
About 11.15

Read the number stories. Write the answers.

1. 3 pens at 10c each. Total cost = [ ]

2. 4 packets containing 3 lollies in each. How many? [ ]

3. 5 children with 3 ice-creams each. Total number of ice-creams? [ ]

4. 6 windows with 3 panes in each. How many panes? [ ]

5. 3 bags containing 8 apples in each. How many apples altogether? [ ]

6. 10 children each scored 3 goals in a game. Total score? [ ]

Draw lines to match the decimals.

8·03   Five-tenths

0·07   Forty-one-hundredths

0·5   Eight and three hundredths

2·63   Five and three-tenths

5·3   Seven-hundredths

0·41   Two and sixty-three-hundredths

S P A C E

The children in class 4K sold tickets for a school play. They kept a tally chart to show the tickets sold.

Tickets Sold	
Adult	𝍸𝍸 𝍸𝍸 𝍸𝍸 IIII
Child	𝍸𝍸 𝍸𝍸 𝍸𝍸 𝍸𝍸 𝍸𝍸 II
Concession	𝍸𝍸 II

1. How many adult tickets were sold? [ ]

2. How many concession tickets were sold? [ ]

3. How many children's tickets were sold? [ ]

4. Which kind of ticket was sold the most? _____

Class 4K then made a column graph to show the tickets sold.

Do the numbers from the tally chart agree with the column graph? [ ]

NUMBER

1. 3 x ☐ = 9
2. 3 x ☐ = 18
3. 3 x ☐ = 24
4. 3 x ☐ = 12
5. 3 x ☐ = 27
6. 3 x ☐ = 15
7. 3 x ☐ = 3
8. 3 x ☐ = 21
9. 3 x ☐ = 30
10. 3 x ☐ = 6

–	18	48	68
7			
5			
9			
6			
4			
8			

Count on in sixes.

0   6   __ __ __ __ __ __ __ __

__ __ __ __ __ __ __

1. 20 + 3 = ☐
2. 76 + 4 = ☐
3. 40 + 6 = ☐
4. 53 + 3 = ☐
5. 88 + 9 = ☐
6. 32 + 8 = ☐
7. 64 + 5 = ☐
8. 43 + 7 = ☐
9. 91 + 6 = ☐
10. 65 + 7 = ☐
11. 82 + 8 = ☐
12. 47 + 6 = ☐
13. 54 + 9 = ☐
14. 38 + 7 = ☐
15. 73 + 2 = ☐

1. 93 + 6 = ☐
2. 58 + 5 = ☐
3. 66 + 8 = ☐
4. 21 + 4 = ☐
5. 47 + 7 = ☐
6. 44 + 2 = ☐
7. 89 + 5 = ☐
8. 68 + 6 = ☐
9. 35 + 4 = ☐
10. 79 + 8 = ☐
11. 53 + 5 = ☐
12. 26 + 7 = ☐
13. 77 + 6 = ☐
14. 71 + 7 = ☐
15. 37 + 9 = ☐

MEASUREMENT

Measure 1 kilogram of rice, flour or sand into a plastic bag and seal it carefully.

Use this kilogram mass to help you put these objects in the correct place in the chart:

a pair of shoes

a telephone book

3 plates

a pillow

2 litres of milk

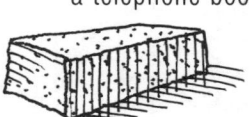
a brick

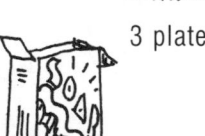
soap powder

a school bag

I hefted these to compare them with a 1 kilogram mass.

Less than 1 kilogram	About 1 kilogram	More than 1 kilogram

1. Write these amounts on the price tickets.

(a) One dollar sixty-three

(b) Four dollars fifty-one

(c) Three dollars eighty

(d) One dollar ten

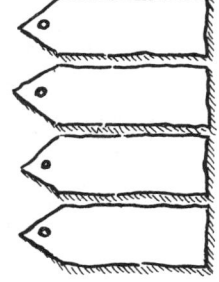

2. Which is the cheapest price?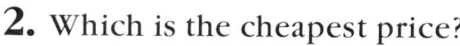

3. Which is the dearest price?

4. Draw and label some coins to show how you could make these amounts.

(a) $1

(b) $0.75

5. From the supermarket find the price and label these articles.

(a)    (b)    (c)

S P A C E

1. How many lines of symmetry do these shapes have? Use a mirror to help you if you need to. Draw the lines of symmetry.

 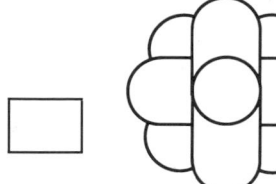 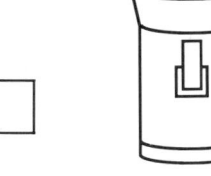 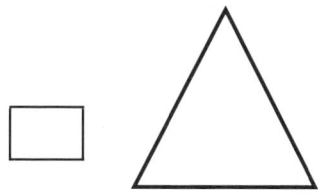 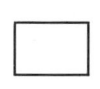

2. Complete these shapes and patterns to make them symmetrical.

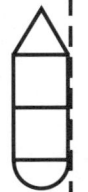   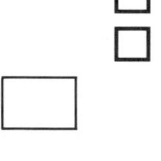 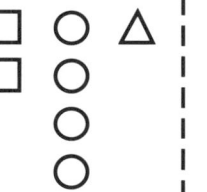 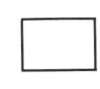

3. Write in the box the number of lines of symmetry each shape has.

4. Name a flag that is symmetrical. _____ Draw it on a piece of paper.

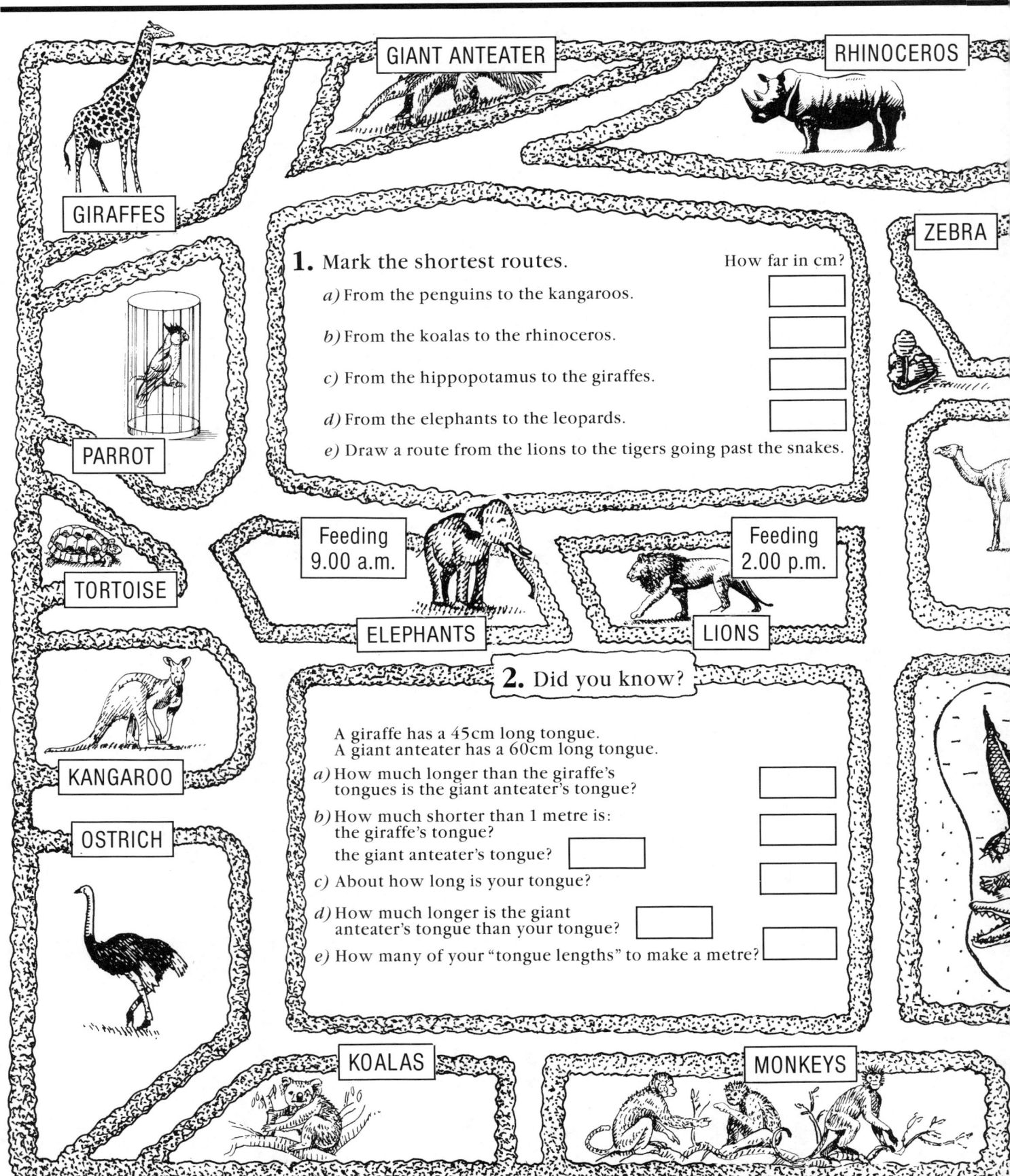

GIANT ANTEATER

RHINOCEROS

GIRAFFES

ZEBRA

PARROT

1. Mark the shortest routes.   How far in cm?

a) From the penguins to the kangaroos.

b) From the koalas to the rhinoceros.

c) From the hippopotamus to the giraffes.

d) From the elephants to the leopards.

e) Draw a route from the lions to the tigers going past the snakes.

TORTOISE

Feeding
9.00 a.m.

ELEPHANTS

Feeding
2.00 p.m.

LIONS

KANGAROO

OSTRICH

2. Did you know?

A giraffe has a 45cm long tongue.
A giant anteater has a 60cm long tongue.

a) How much longer than the giraffe's
tongues is the giant anteater's tongue?

b) How much shorter than 1 metre is:
the giraffe's tongue?
the giant anteater's tongue?

c) About how long is your tongue?

d) How much longer is the giant
anteater's tongue than your tongue?

e) How many of your "tongue lengths" to make a metre?

KOALAS

MONKEYS

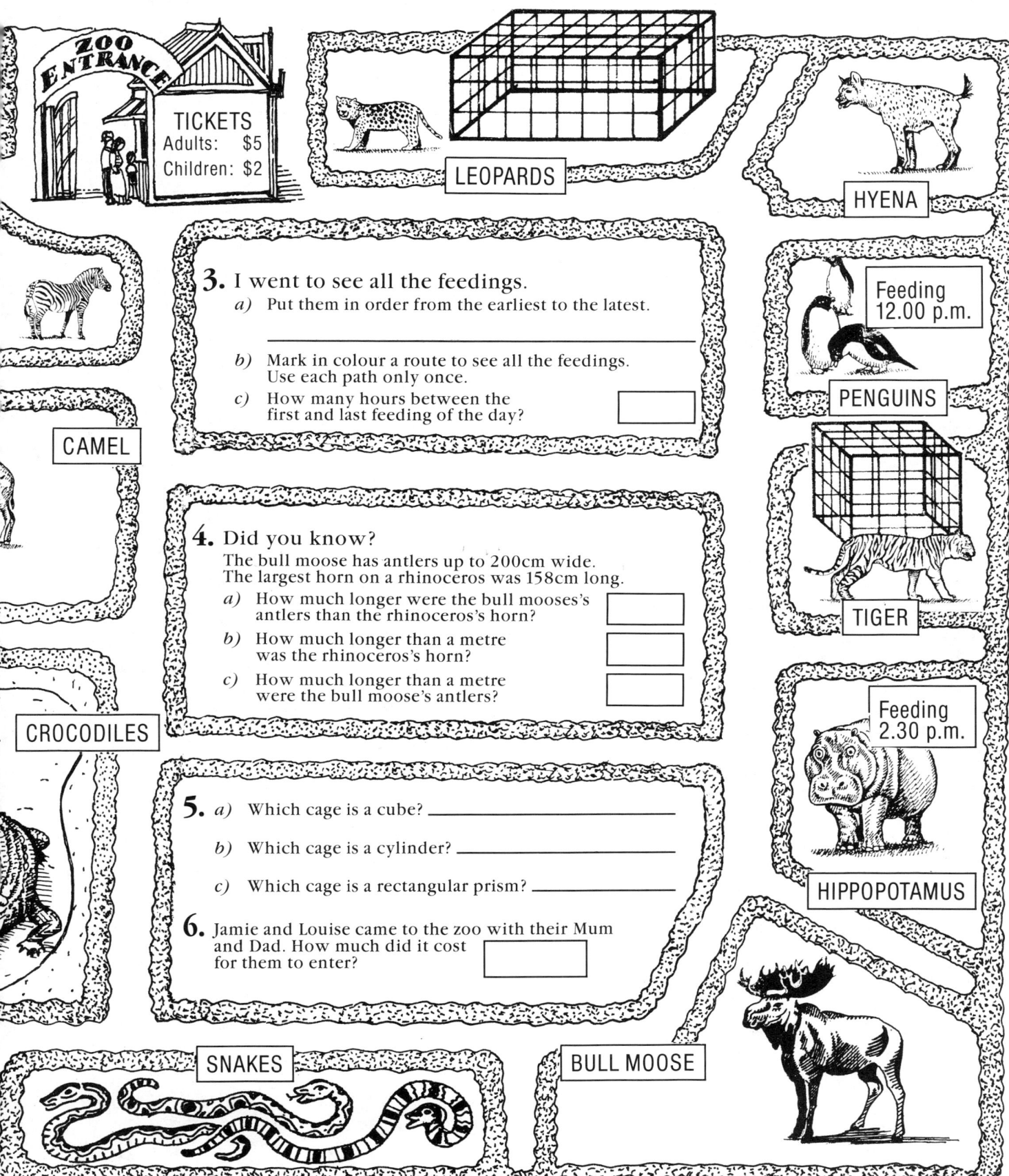

ZOO ENTRANCE

TICKETS
Adults: $5
Children: $2

LEOPARDS

HYENA

Feeding 12.00 p.m.

PENGUINS

ZEBRA

CAMEL

3. I went to see all the feedings.

a) Put them in order from the earliest to the latest.

_____

b) Mark in colour a route to see all the feedings.
Use each path only once.

c) How many hours between the
first and last feeding of the day?

TIGER

4. **Did you know?**
The bull moose has antlers up to 200cm wide.
The largest horn on a rhinoceros was 158cm long.

a) How much longer were the bull mooses's
antlers than the rhinoceros's horn?

b) How much longer than a metre
was the rhinoceros's horn?

c) How much longer than a metre
were the bull moose's antlers?

Feeding 2.30 p.m.

CROCODILES

HIPPOPOTAMUS

5. *a)* Which cage is a cube? _____

b) Which cage is a cylinder? _____

c) Which cage is a rectangular prism? _____

6. Jamie and Louise came to the zoo with their Mum
and Dad. How much did it cost
for them to enter?

SNAKES

BULL MOOSE

NUMBER

Complete these.

6 x 1 = ☐

6 x 2 = ☐

6 x 3 = ☐

6 x 4 = ☐

6 x 5 = ☐

6 x 6 = ☐

6 x 7 = ☐

6 x 8 = ☐

6 x 9 = ☐

6 x 10 = ☐

You will need to use Base 10 blocks to work these out.

1. To put 120 apples onto trays, with 20 apples to a tray, how many trays are needed? ☐

2. 96 eggs had to go in cartons of 12. How many cartons? ☐

Count on in nines.

0 __ __ __ __ __ __ __

__ __ __ __ __ __

__ __ __ __ __ __

1. 3 x 3 = ☐

2. 4 x ☐ = 12

3. ☐ x 3 = 6

4. 3 x 8 = ☐

5. 3 x 6 = ☐

6. ☐ x 3 = 27

7. 3 x ☐ = 24

8. 3 x ☐ = 15

9. 8 x 3 = ☐

10. ☐ x 4 = 12

11. 3 x 9 = ☐

12. 3 x ☐ = 21

13. 3 x 4 = ☐

14. ☐ x 10 = 30

1. 90 – 8 = ☐

2. 55 – 7 = ☐

3. 64 – 9 = ☐

4. 47 – 5 = ☐

5. 78 – 6 = ☐

6. 80 – 8 = ☐

7. 25 – 5 = ☐

8. 69 – 7 = ☐

9. 74 – 3 = ☐

10. 37 – 7 = ☐

11. 86 – 6 = ☐

12. 88 – 5 = ☐

13. 35 – 6 = ☐

14. 77 – 4 = ☐

MEASUREMENT

Make a 1 litre container – here's how. Measure exactly 1 litre of water into a milk carton. Carefully mark the level, empty the carton and cut off above the marked level. Use your 1 litre container to check the capacity of these items.

Fill out the chart by placing the items in the correct column.

Less than 1 litre	About 1 litre	More than 1 litre

Complete this chart.

How many litres in ...	Estimate	Measured
a garbage bin?		
a sink?		
a kettle?		

How many drops in 1 litre?

How would you find out?

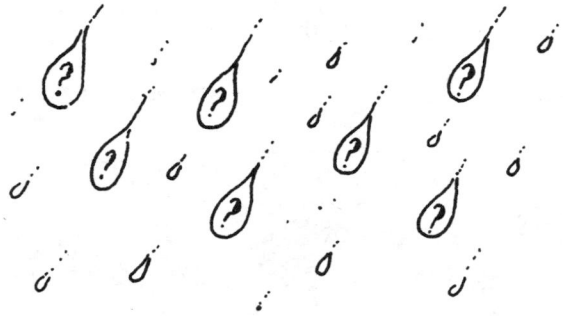

1. A thousand is made up of ☐ [flat] or ☐ [rod] or ☐ [cube]

2. How many more [flat] to make 1000? ☐

3. How many more [rod] to make 1000? ☐

4. How many more [cube] to make 1000? ☐

5. [cube + 2 flats] = ☐ thousand and ☐ hundreds = ☐

6. [2 cubes, 2 flats, 2 rods] = ☐ thousands, ☐ hundreds and ☐ tens = ☐

7. 2864 = ☐ thousands, ☐ hundreds, ☐ tens and ☐ ones

8. 4579 = ☐ thousands, ☐ hundreds, ☐ tens and ☐ ones

S P A C E

In the boxes below each shape draw the cross-sections each shape would show if cut on the broken lines.

1)	2)	3)	4)	5)	6)

Now name each shape you've drawn.

1) _____ 2) _____ 3) _____ 4) _____ 5) _____ 6) _____

UNIT 7

▲▲▲▲▲

N U M B E R

Complete these.

9 x 1 = ☐   6 x ☐ = 12   Double 8 = ☐

9 x 2 = ☐   6 x ☐ = 24

9 x 3 = ☐   6 x ☐ = 36   Double 10 = ☐

9 x 4 = ☐   6 x ☐ = 48

9 x 5 = ☐   6 x ☐ = 6   Double 20 = ☐

9 x 6 = ☐   6 x ☐ = 54

9 x 7 = ☐   6 x ☐ = 42   Double 50 = ☐

9 x 8 = ☐   6 x ☐ = 18

9 x 9 = ☐   6 x ☐ = 30   Double 100 = ☐

9 x 10 = ☐   6 x ☐ = 0

9 x 0 = ☐   6 x ☐ = 60

Use Base 10 blocks to work out this: 200 pegs are to be packed into packets with 25 pegs in each. How many packets will there be? ☐

1. ☐ x 3 = 3	1. 40 ÷ 2 = ☐
2. 3 x ☐ = 30	2. 28 ÷ 2 = ☐
3. 3 x 4 = ☐	3. 69 ÷ 2 = ☐
4. 3 x 2 = ☐	4. 57 ÷ 2 = ☐
5. 3 x ☐ = 15	5. 30 ÷ 2 = ☐
6. 3 x ☐ = 21	6. 88 ÷ 2 = ☐
7. 6 x ☐ = 18	7. 20 ÷ 2 = ☐
8. 3 x ☐ = 24	8. 49 ÷ 2 = ☐
9. ☐ x 6 = 18	9. 58 ÷ 2 = ☐
10. 3 x 7 = ☐	10. 68 ÷ 2 = ☐
11. ☐ x 5 = 15	11. 70 ÷ 2 = ☐
12. 3 x 9 = ☐	12. 76 ÷ 2 = ☐
13. 3 x ☐ = 12	13. ☐ ÷ 2 = 41
14. ☐ x 5 = 15	14. ☐ ÷ 2 = 60
15. 2 x 6 = ☐	15. ☐ ÷ 2 = 72
16. ☐ x 1 = 3	16. ☐ ÷ 2 = 91

▲▲

M E A S U R E M E N T

Which one is hotter? Circle the hotter thermometer.

1) 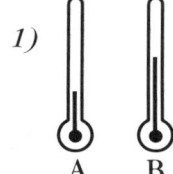    2) 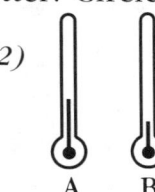 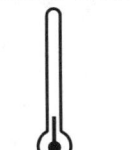   3) 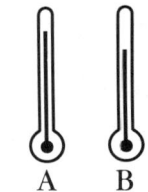    4)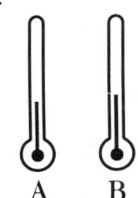

A   B   A   B   A   B   A   B

The thermometers below show temperatures during the day. Write a word to describe the temperature.

_____   _____   _____

What time of day do you think it is when the temperature is like this?

_____   _____   _____

This is the temperature if the thermometer is put into cold milk. What will happen if you put this into hot coffee?

_____
_____

Show this on the thermometer below.

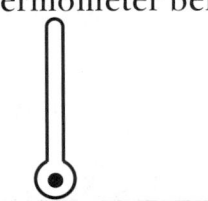

16

• • • • •

Draw Base 10 blocks to show these numbers:

1. One thousand, two hundred and thirty-seven.

2. Three thousand, five hundred and twenty-nine.

Write these numbers.

1.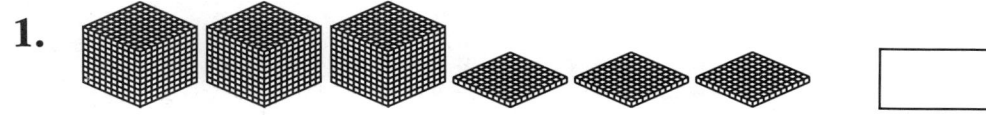

2.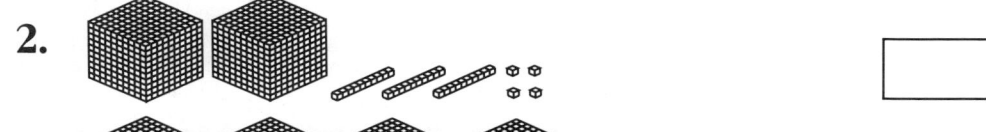

3.

S P A C E

These shapes are all  . Match the name with the shape.

Write the name of the shape of
each base in the box beneath it.

1. [   ]

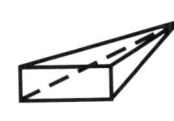

2. [   ]

Square Pyramid

Pentagonal Pyramid

Hexagonal Pyramid

Rectangular Pyramid

Triangular Pyramid

3. [   ]

4. [   ]

5. [   ]

One place where I could see a pyramid is _____

NUMBER

Complete this
Addition Crossnumber Puzzle.

Across
1. $22 + 35 =$ 5. $32 + 35 =$
2. $47 + 12 =$ 7. $11 + 66 =$
4. $60 + 30 =$ 8. $13 + 44 =$

Down
1. $28 + 30 =$ 4. $63 + 31 =$
2. $25 + 25 =$ 6. $15 + 60 =$
3. $41 + 26 =$ 7. $42 + 36 =$

Complete these.

$9 \times \boxed{} = 9$

$9 \times \boxed{} = 36$

$9 \times \boxed{} = 54$

$9 \times \boxed{} = 81$

$9 \times \boxed{} = 27$

$9 \times \boxed{} = 63$

$9 \times \boxed{} = 72$

$9 \times \boxed{} = 90$

$9 \times \boxed{} = 45$

$9 \times \boxed{} = 18$

1. $6 \times 1 = \square$ 1. $60 + 4 = \square$
2. $6 \times 4 = \square$ 2. $47 + 4 = \square$
3. $6 \times 8 = \square$ 3. $78 + 4 = \square$
4. $6 \times 5 = \square$ 4. $96 + 4 = \square$
5. $6 \times 10 = \square$ 5. $39 + 4 = \square$
6. $6 \times 6 = \square$ 6. $55 + 4 = \square$
7. $6 \times 2 = \square$ 7. $24 + 4 = \square$
8. $6 \times 7 = \square$ 8. $69 + \square = 73$
9. $6 \times 9 = \square$ 9. $77 + 4 = \square$
10. $6 \times 0 = \square$ 10. $28 + \square = 32$
11. $6 \times 3 = \square$ 11. $86 + 4 = \square$
12. $6 \times 6 = \square$ 12. $95 + 4 = \square$
13. $6 \times 10 = \square$ 13. $38 + 4 = \square$
14. $6 \times 8 = \square$ 14. $57 + \square = 61$
15. $6 \times 4 = \square$ 15. $79 + 4 = \square$
16. $6 \times 5 = \square$ 16. $56 + 4 = \square$
17. $6 \times 9 = \square$ 17. $\square + 4 = 54$
18. $6 \times 7 = \square$ 18. $\square + 4 = 82$

▲▲

MEASUREMENT

Join sheets of newspaper together with glue or tape to make a square metre.

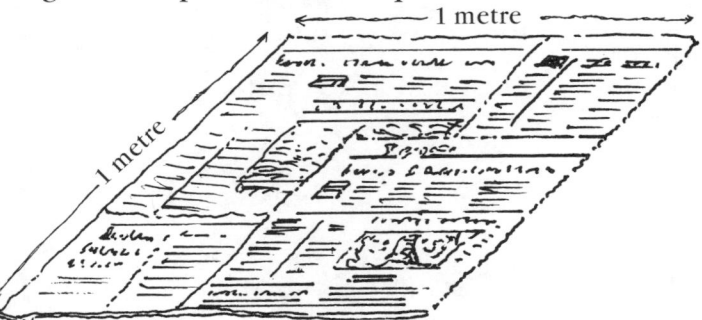

← 1 metre →

1 metre

Use your class or your family to find out:
How many people can fit on a square metre?

standing $\boxed{}$ sitting $\boxed{}$ lying down $\boxed{}$

Find items in your classroom, school or house which have areas smaller or larger than one square metre. Complete this table.

Area smaller than a square metre	Area larger than a square metre

1. Twenty-hundredths are shaded.

_____ tenths are shaded.

2. Forty-hundredths are shaded.

Four_____ are shaded.

3. _____

_____

4. _____

_____

5. _____

_____

6. _____

_____

Who am I?

I am a 2-digit number.
I am a multiple of 3.
I am a multiple of 5.
I am between 25 and 35.

Who am I? [ ]

I am even.
I am a multiple of 3.
I am a multiple of 7.
I am between 40 and 45.

Who am I? [ ]

S P A C E

A	B	C	D

Mark 4 routes to move the dog into the kennel.

1. Which route is the shortest? _____ How many squares? [ ]

2. Which route is the longest? _____ How many squares? [ ]

This dog is lost. Draw the shortest path to the kennel but don't go past the butcher shops!

UNIT 9

▲▲▲▲▲

Solve these number stories. Write the algorithm and answer in the boxes.

1. Ali had saved $55 but he wanted to buy a game worth $78. How much did he still have to save?

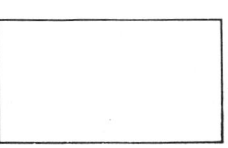

2. 38 children travelled by bus. At the high school 16 got off. How many children were left on the bus?

3. 44 people were in the hall to see the concert. 23 of these were children. How many were adults?

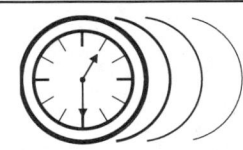

1. 6 x 6 = ☐
2. 6 x ☐ = 48
3. 6 x 1 = ☐
4. 6 x ☐ = 54
5. 6 x 0 = ☐
6. 6 x 7 = ☐
7. 6 x ☐ = 24
8. 6 x ☐ = 60
9. ☐ x 6 = 30
10. ☐ x 3 = 18
11. 6 x 9 = ☐
12. 6 x ☐ = 30
13. 6 x 8 = ☐
14. 6 x 6 = ☐
15. 6 x ☐ = 42
16. ☐ x 4 = 24
17. 6 x ☐ = 48
18. ☐ x 6 = 6

1. 68 + 3 = ☐
2. 57 + 3 = ☐
3. 89 + 3 = ☐
4. 46 + 3 = ☐
5. 39 + 3 = ☐
6. 87 + 3 = ☐
7. 58 + 3 = ☐
8. 79 + 3 = ☐
9. 36 + 3 = ☐
10. 60 + 3 = ☐
11. 29 + 3 = ☐
12. 78 + 3 = ☐
13. ☐ + 3 = 62
14. ☐ + 3 = 30
15. ☐ + 3 = 51
16. ☐ + 3 = 60
17. ☐ + 3 = 82
18. ☐ + 3 = 91

▲▲

Estimate and measure in metres or centimetres.

	Estimate	Measured
length of desk		
width of desk		
length of shoe		
hand span		
perimeter of desk top		
length of left thumbnail		
width of your pen or pencil		

	Estimate	Measured
the thickness of your desk top		
distance around forehead		
distance around your wrist		
your height		
your reach		
your pace		
distance to the blackboard		

Which was the greatest distance? _____

Which was the smallest? _____

1. Write the answer as a decimal.

(a) 3 tenths and 5 hundredths = ☐

(b) 6 tenths and 15 hundredths = ☐

(c) 7 tenths and 12 hundredths = ☐

(d) 9 tenths and 10 hundredths = ☐

(e) 3 tenths and 15 hundredths = ☐

2. Circle and colour the larger number.

(a) 8 tenths   or   65 hundredths

(b) 16 hundredths   or   6 tenths and 1 hundredth

(c) 5 tenths   or   5 hundredths

(d) 7 tenths   or   69 hundredths

3. Complete these wheels.

(a)
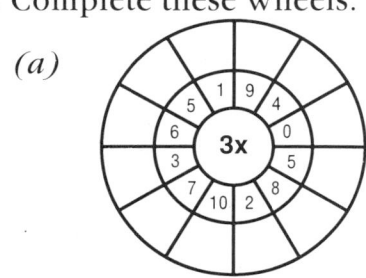

(b)

(c)
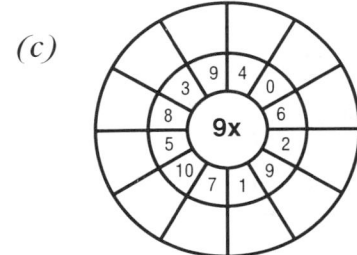

SPACE

2. Draw:

1.

My angle	Make an angle that is:		
	Smaller	The same size	Larger
⌐			
▷			

3. Match the angles that are the same.

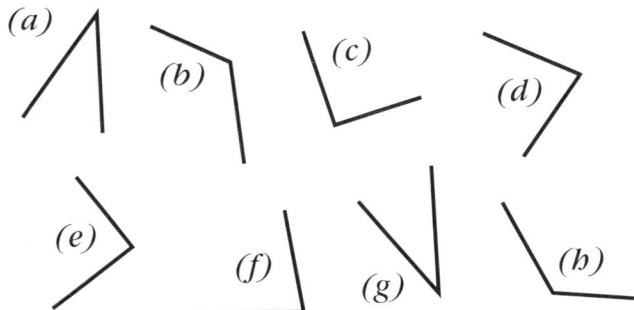

A blunt angle
A sharp angle
A large angle
A small angle
A straight angle

Fairytales
• • • • • • • • • •

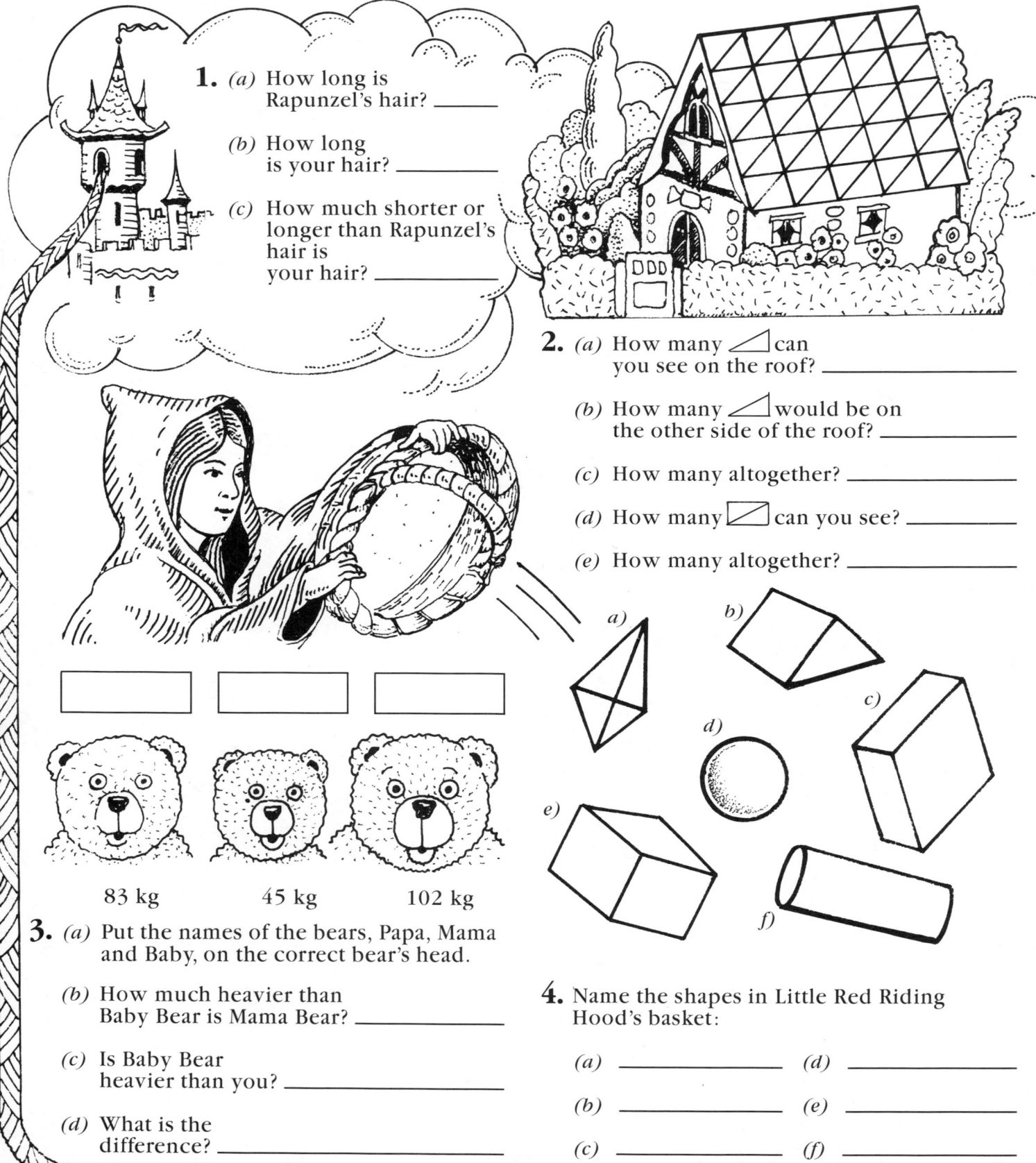

1. *(a)* How long is Rapunzel's hair? _____

(b) How long is your hair? _____

(c) How much shorter or longer than Rapunzel's hair is your hair? _____

2. *(a)* How many ◁ can you see on the roof? _____

(b) How many ◁ would be on the other side of the roof? _____

(c) How many altogether? _____

(d) How many ▱ can you see? _____

(e) How many altogether? _____

a)
b)
c)
d)
e)
f)

83 kg   45 kg   102 kg

3. *(a)* Put the names of the bears, Papa, Mama and Baby, on the correct bear's head.

(b) How much heavier than Baby Bear is Mama Bear? _____

(c) Is Baby Bear heavier than you? _____

(d) What is the difference? _____

4. Name the shapes in Little Red Riding Hood's basket:

(a) _____   *(d)* _____

(b) _____   *(e)* _____

(c) _____   *(f)* _____

Fee! Fi! Fo! Fum!
I smell the blood of
an English man.
Be he alive or
be he dead
I'll grind his bones
to make my bread.

5. (a) Which letter appears most? _____

Which letters appear least? _____

(b) What is the difference between the letter which appears most and those which appear least? _____

6 + 7 =	16 + 7 =	26 + 7 =	36 + 7 =
8 + 3 =	18 + 3 =	28 + 3 =	38 + 3 =
4 + 9 =	14 + 9 =	24 + 9 =	34 + 9 =
3 + 4 =	13 + 4 =	23 + 4 =	33 + 4 =
7 + 2 =	17 + 2 =	27 + 2 =	37 + 2 =

6. (a) How many bricks altogether in Humpty's wall? _____

(b) Answer the questions in each brick.

7. The beanstalk grew 9 m in 1 day.

(a) How many metres did it grow in 3 days? _____

(b) How many metres did it grow in 6 days? _____

(c) How many metres did it grow in 9 days? _____

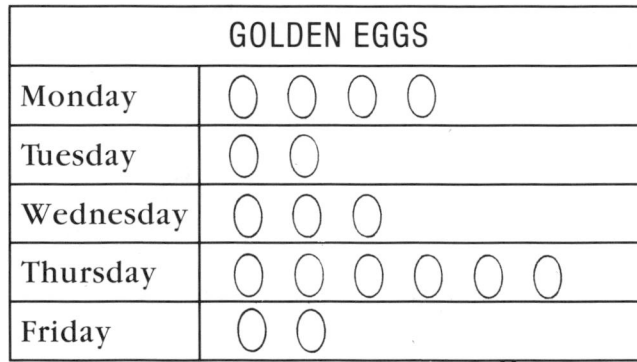

GOLDEN EGGS	
Monday	O O O O
Tuesday	O O
Wednesday	O O O
Thursday	O O O O O O
Friday	O O

8. (a) On which day were the most eggs laid? _____

(b) On which days were the least laid? _____

_____

(c) On which day were three eggs laid? _____

(d) How many eggs altogether? _____

NUMBER

1. Can you write a x and ÷ number sentence for this array?

● ● ● ● ● ●

● ● ● ● ● ●

● ● ● ● ● ●

☐
☐

2. Now write in a x or ÷ number sentence to match the one given.

(a) 3 x 5 = 15 ☐

(b) 30 ÷ 6 = ☐ ☐

(c) 4 x 6 = ☐ ☐

(d) 21 ÷ 3 = ☐ ☐

(e) 7 x 6 = ☐ ☐

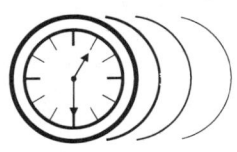

1. 9 x 2 = ☐   1. 30 – 2 = ☐
2. 9 x 4 = ☐   2. 61 – 2 = ☐
3. 9 x 0 = ☐   3. 42 – 2 = ☐
4. 9 x 3 = ☐   4. 21 – 2 = ☐
5. 9 x 1 = ☐   5. 33 – 2 = ☐
6. 9 x 5 = ☐   6. 81 – 2 = ☐
7. 9 x 8 = ☐   7. 92 – 2 = ☐
8. 9 x 6 = ☐   8. 55 – 2 = ☐
9. 9 x 9 = ☐   9. 67 – 2 = ☐
10. 9 x 7 = ☐   10. ☐ – 2 = 56
11. 9 x 9 = ☐   11. ☐ – 2 = 28
12. 9 x 6 = ☐   12. ☐ – 2 = 69
13. 7 x 9 = ☐   13. ☐ – 2 = 80
14. 9 x 8 = ☐   14. ☐ – 2 = 78
15. 5 x 9 = ☐   15. ☐ – 2 = 30
16. 6 x 9 = ☐   16. ☐ – 2 = 44

MEASUREMENT

Here is the timetable for Emu Primary School.

9.15a.m.	Assembly	12.30p.m.	Lunch
9.30a.m.	Lessons start	1.30p.m.	Lessons
11.00a.m.	Recess	3.15p.m.	Lessons end
11.20a.m.	Lessons		

Write out your school's timetable.

1. How long does Assembly take? _____

2. How long is recess? _____

3. How long is lunch? _____

4. How long are the morning lessons? _____

5. How long are the afternoon lessons? _____

6. Which session of lessons is the longest? _____

7. How long is the school day? _____

8. How long is spent on lessons? _____

Now answer the questions using your school's timetable.

Write these numbers.

1.

2.

3.

4.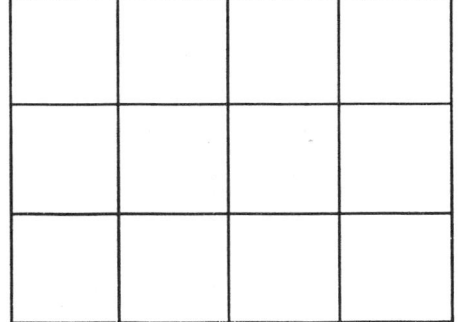

5.

1. 3 x 6 = ☐
2. 6 x ☐ = 24
3. 3 x 9 = ☐
4. 4 x ☐ = 36
5. 6 x ☐ = 18
6. 6 x 6 = ☐
7. 8 x ☐ = 48
8. 8 x ☐ = 24
9. 7 x ☐ = 42
10. 5 x ☐ = 30
11. 5 x ☐ = 45
12. 3 x 8 = ☐
13. 6 x ☐ = 54

SPACE

1. (a) How many squares? ☐
    Colour these squares using 2 colours.

(b) Are there any gaps? ☐
    These shapes tessellate.

2. (a) How many triangles? ☐

(b) How many rectangles? ☐
    Colour using 2 colours.

(c) Are there any gaps? ☐
    These shapes tessellate.

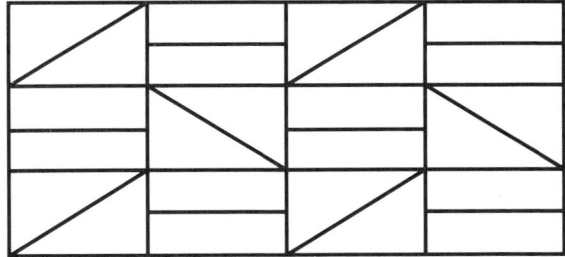

3. Do these shapes tessellate? ☐

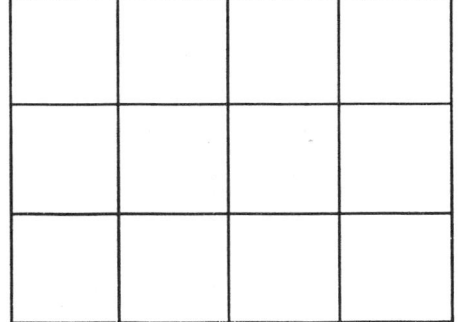

4. Do these shapes tessellate? ☐

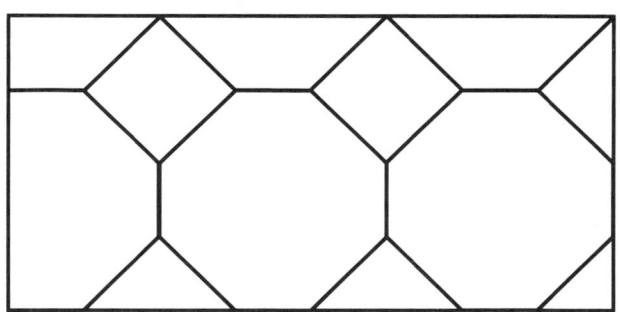

NUMBER

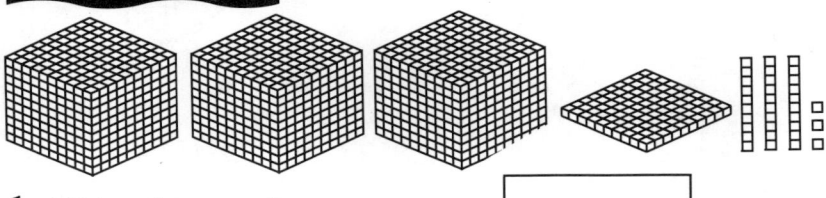

1. Write this number: [   ]

    (a) How many thousands? [   ]

    (b) How many hundreds? [   ]

    (c) How many tens? [   ]

    (d) How many ones? [   ]

2. What value has 7 in:

    (a) 7492?_____

    (b) 9170?_____

    (c) 2761?_____

    (d) 5347?_____

1. $9 \times 9 = \square$
2. $9 \times \square = 9$
3. $9 \times 4 = \square$
4. $\square \times 9 = 18$
5. $9 \times \square = 54$
6. $\square \times 9 = 27$
7. $9 \times \square = 18$
8. $9 \times 5 = \square$
9. $9 \times \square = 63$
10. $\square \times 9 = 0$
11. $\square \times 9 = 81$
12. $9 \times \square = 72$
13. $9 \times \square = 45$
14. $9 \times 7 = \square$
15. $9 \times 8 = \square$

1. $60 - 4 = \square$
2. $72 - 4 = \square$
3. $91 - 4 = \square$
4. $53 - 4 = \square$
5. $30 - 4 = \square$
6. $82 - 4 = \square$
7. $33 - 4 = \square$
8. $61 - 4 = \square$
9. $20 - 4 = \square$
10. $\square - 4 = 46$
11. $\square - 4 = 88$
12. $\square - 4 = 30$
13. $\square - 4 = 57$
14. $\square - 4 = 76$
15. $\square - 4 = 20$

MEASUREMENT

Make a ½ kilogram mass. You can do this by making another 1 kilogram bag of sand, flour or rice then splitting it into 2 equal bags. Find 3 objects for each column in this table:

Less than ½ kilogram	Between ½ kilogram and 1 kilogram	More than 1 kilogram

Try these:

How many of these make ½ kilogram?	Estimate	Check
oranges apples knives and forks Lego pieces flats		

To check you can use a

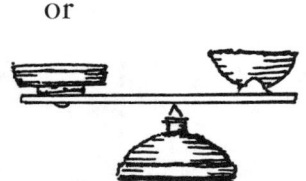 or 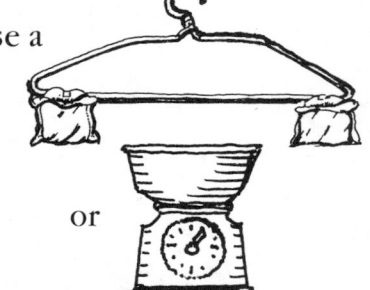 or

Write these numbers.

1. Five thousand, two hundred and fifty-one

2. Seven thousand, nine hundred

3. Six thousand and four

4. Eight thousand, one hundred and nine

5. Five thousand, four hundred and sixty

Write a ÷ or × number sentence to match the one given.

1. $24 \div 3 = \square$

2. $6 \times 10 = \square$

3. $6 \times \square = 36$

4. $45 \div 9 = \square$

1. Round off these to the nearest hundred.

3690

5717

2. Round off these to the nearest ten.

684

1127

SPACE

Draw a line to match the net with the shape.

1.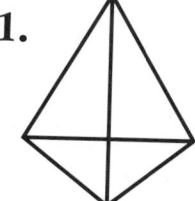

2.

3.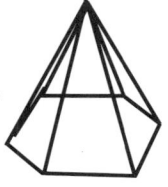

(c)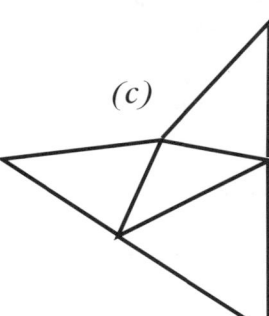

(a)

4.

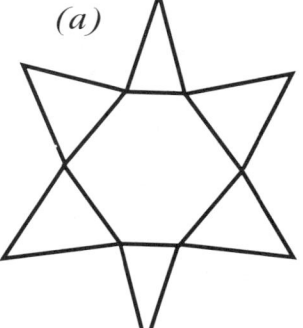

(b)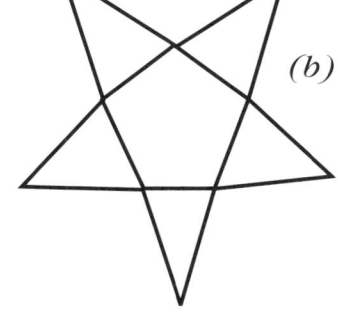

(d)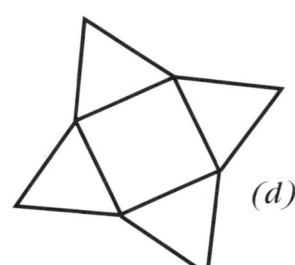

N U M B E R

 9c    8c    5c    15c

Fruit Shop

1. How much would one piece of each fruit cost altogether?

2. What is the difference in price between the cheapest and the dearest piece of fruit?

3. Special deal

3 for 25c, 4  for 50c

Which is the better buy? _____

4. A bag of bananas normally costs $1.20. A sale reduced its price by half. What does a bag cost now?

1. 6 x 8 = ☐
2. 3 x 10 = ☐
3. 6 x ☐ = 54
4. 3 x ☐ = 24
5. 6 x 7 = ☐
6. ☐ x 7 = 21
7. 6 x ☐ = 36
8. 3 x ☐ = 27
9. ☐ x 6 = 30
10. 3 x 5 = ☐
11. 6 x 4 = ☐
12. 3 x ☐ = 18
13. ☐ x 6 = 48
14. 3 x ☐ = 15
15. 6 x ☐ = 54
16. 3 x 3 = ☐

1. 60 – 3 = ☐
2. 91 – 3 = ☐
3. 43 – 3 = ☐
4. 80 – 3 = ☐
5. 52 – 3 = ☐
6. 71 – 3 = ☐
7. 33 – 3 = ☐
8. 64 – 3 = ☐
9. 21 – 3 = ☐
10. ☐ – 3 = 40
11. ☐ – 3 = 29
12. ☐ – 3 = 68
13. ☐ – 3 = 37
14. ☐ – 3 = 70
15. ☐ – 3 = 90
16. ☐ – 3 = 58

M E A S U R E M E N T

Use the square metre you made in Unit 8 to measure some rooms in your house or school.

Room	Estimate in square metres	Measurement in square metres
A		
B		
C		
D		
E		

1. Which room was the biggest? _____

2. How much bigger was it than the smallest room? _____

3. When measuring did you have many parts of a square metre? _____ Did this make measuring more difficult?

Why? _____

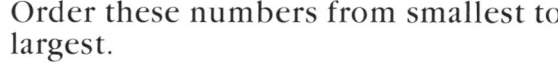
Circle the larger number in blue, and the smaller number in red.

1. 4600   4069

2. 3333   3033

3. 7899   7988

4. 5050   5100

Order these numbers from smallest to largest.

| 6990 | 6970 | 6980 | 6960 |

_____

| 3500 | 3100 | 3400 | 3200 |

_____

Make this number on your calculator. Now add just one number to make your calculator read 3778.

What number did you add? [ ]

Try these:

Key in:	Add:	To make:
4072		4872
3805		3895
6020		6222

▲▲

S P A C E

A Playground Map

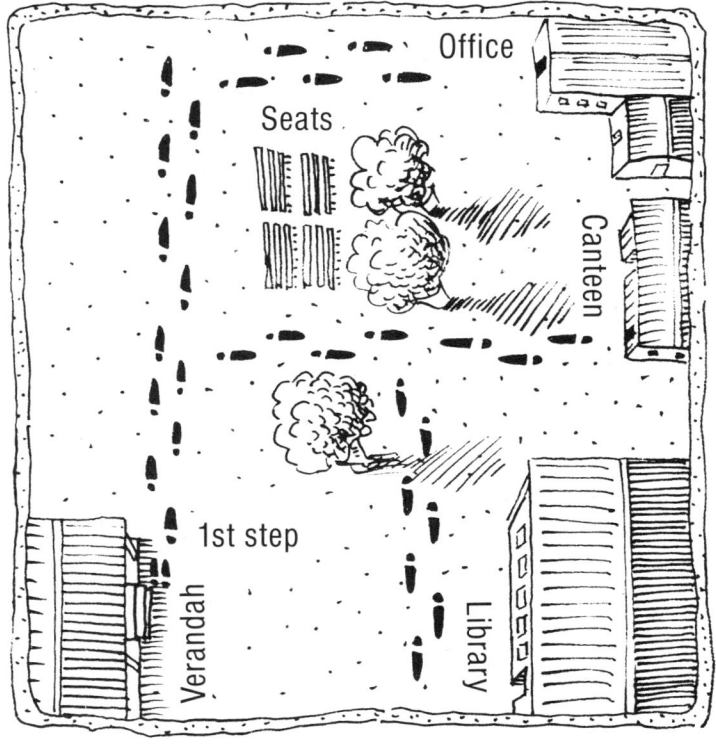

1. Turn left at the bottom of the verandah steps and walk six steps. Turn right and walk four steps. Turn right and walk seven steps.
   Where are you? _____

2. Turn left at the bottom of the verandah steps and walk twelve steps. Turn right and walk five steps.
   Where are you? _____

3. Write directions to get to the canteen from the library.

_____

_____

_____

_____

N U M B E R

1. Count on in eights.

0 __ __ __ __ __ __ __ __ __

__ __ __ __ __ __ __ __ __

2. Now complete these.

8 x 1 = ☐   8 x 2 = ☐   8 x 3 = ☐   8 x 4 = ☐

8 x 5 = ☐   8 x 6 = ☐   8 x 7 = ☐   8 x 8 = ☐

8 x 9 = ☐   8 x 10 = ☐

3. What number comes before these numbers?

8647 ☐   3330 ☐

7100 ☐   5000 ☐

4. What number comes after these numbers?

8600 ☐   7959 ☐

6666 ☐   3999 ☐

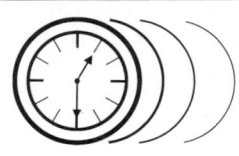

1. 6 x 8 = ☐   1. 70 + 5 = ☐
2. 9 x 10 = ☐   2. 39 + 5 = ☐
3. 6 x ☐ = 54   3. 86 + 5 = ☐
4. 9 x ☐ = 81   4. 57 + 5 = ☐
5. 6 x 7 = ☐   5. 35 + 5 = ☐
6. ☐ x 7 = 63   6. 68 + 5 = ☐
7. 9 x ☐ = 72   7. 25 + 5 = ☐
8. 6 x ☐ = 36   8. 67 + 5 = ☐
9. ☐ x 6 = 30   9. 88 + 5 = ☐
10. 9 x 5 = ☐   10. 46 + 5 = ☐
11. 6 x 4 = ☐   11. 71 + 5 = ☐
12. 9 x ☐ = 36   12. 24 + 5 = ☐
13. ☐ x 6 = 48   13. ☐ + 5 = 64
14. 9 x ☐ = 9   14. ☐ + 5 = 81
15. 6 x ☐ = 54   15. ☐ + 5 = 42
16. 9 x 3 = ☐   16. ☐ + 5 = 93
17. 6 x ☐ = 0   17. ☐ + 5 = 40

M E A S U R E M E N T

1. Some children measured their heights and made a chart to show the results.

Finish the chart for them:

Children	Height		
Nick	126 cm	1 m 26cm	1.26 m
Jane	110 cm		
Ivan		1 m 31 cm	
George			1.15 m
Lee	169 cm		
Maria		1 m 22 cm	

2. *(a)* Who was the tallest? _____

(b) Who was the shortest? _____

(c) How much bigger than Ivan was Lee? _____

(d) Maria's little sister is 89cm. How much taller is Maria? _____

(e) If Jane stood on Lee's shoulders and Ivan stood on Nick's shoulders, which pair would be taller?

_____

By how much? _____

1. Shade $\frac{2}{10}$ or $\frac{20}{100}$

2. Shade $\frac{70}{100}$.
Another name is ⬚ .

3. Colour 1 tenth more than 5 tenths.

4. Colour 30 hundredths green and 1 tenth blue.
Altogether ⬚ tenths are coloured.

5. Colour 80 hundredths yellow and 1 tenth red.
Altogether ⬚ tenths are coloured.

6. *(a)* 7 tenths of one dollar is ⬚ .

(b) 70 hundredths of one dollar is ⬚ .

(c) How many more tenths to make a dollar? ⬚

7. Count on

in tens: 3010 ____ ____ ____ ____ ____ ____

and in sixes: 4012 ____ ____ ____ ____ ____

▲▲▲

S P A C E

1. Trace around a 5c coin. Cover the shape above with circles. The circles should all touch.
Are there any gaps? ⬚
Circles do not tessellate.

2. Make a tiling pattern using squares and triangles to make tessellating shapes. The dots may help you.

3. Can you find any tessellating shapes in your home? Write them here.

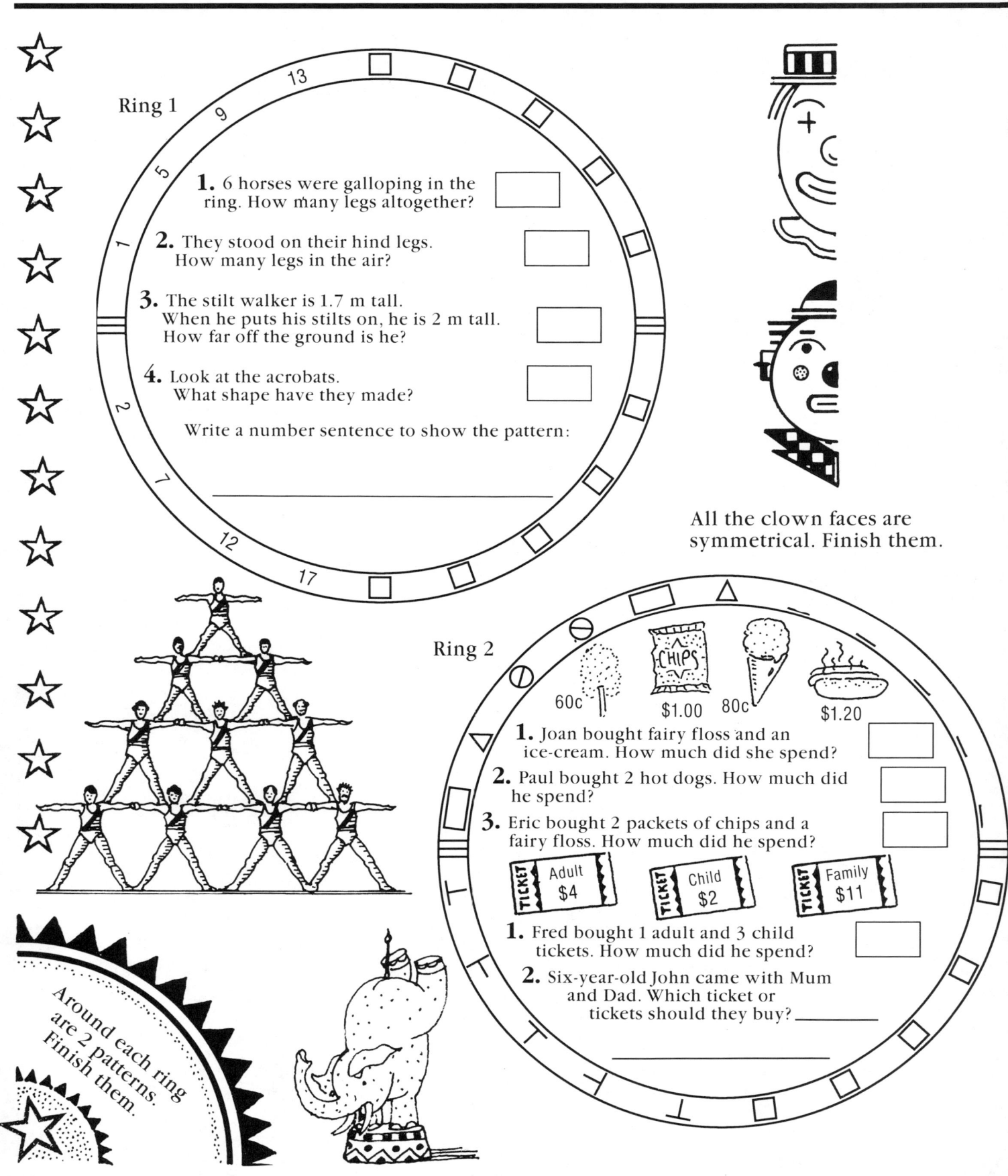

Ring 1

13
9
5
1
2
7
12
17

1. 6 horses were galloping in the ring. How many legs altogether?

2. They stood on their hind legs. How many legs in the air?

3. The stilt walker is 1.7 m tall. When he puts his stilts on, he is 2 m tall. How far off the ground is he?

4. Look at the acrobats. What shape have they made?

Write a number sentence to show the pattern:

_____

All the clown faces are symmetrical. Finish them.

Ring 2

60c $1.00 80c $1.20

1. Joan bought fairy floss and an ice-cream. How much did she spend?

2. Paul bought 2 hot dogs. How much did he spend?

3. Eric bought 2 packets of chips and a fairy floss. How much did he spend?

Adult $4   Child $2   Family $11

1. Fred bought 1 adult and 3 child tickets. How much did he spend?

2. Six-year-old John came with Mum and Dad. Which ticket or tickets should they buy? _____

_____

Around each ring are 2 patterns. Finish them.

ANSWERS

UNIT 1
NUMBER Page 4
Add these:
1. 78 **2.** 68 **3.** 89 **4.** 68
Place values:
1. 6 tens **2.** 1 hundred **3.** 3 ones
4. 4 hundreds

Page 5
Numeral Expander:
1. 253 **2.** 909 **3.** 690 **4.** 164 **5.** 507
6. 378
Smallest to largest:
278 282 286 290 294 298 302
306

UNIT 2
NUMBER Page 6
1. Count on in 3s:
0 3 6 9 12 15 18 21 24 27 30
33 36 39 42 45 48 51 54 57
2. 3 6 9 12 15 18 21 24 27 30
3. Distance differences:
(a) 14 km (b) 13 km (c) 6 km
4. Age differences:
(a) 5 years (b) 9 years (c) 5 years

MEASUREMENT
Areas: **1.** 18 squares **2.** 17 hexagons
3. 36 triangles **4.** 8 L-shapes
Shapes 1, 3 and 4 would be good for
measuring a desktop. Shapes 2, 5 and
6 would not, because they do not fit
together (tessellate).

UNIT 3
NUMBER Page 8
Number pattern:
43 27 55 34
33 17 45 24
25 9 37 16
35 19 47 26

Page 9
Number stories:
1. 30c **2.** 12 **3.** 15 **4.** 18 **5.** 24 **6.** 30
Matching decimals:
8.03 Eight and three-hundredths,
0.07 Seven-hundredths, 0.5 Five-tenths,
2.63 Two and sixty-three hundredths,
5.3 Five and three-tenths,
0.41 Forty-one hundredths
SPACE
1. 19 **2.** 7 **3.** 27 **4.** child

UNIT 4
NUMBER Page 10
1. 3 **2.** 6 **3.** 8 **4.** 4 **5.** 9 **6.** 5 **7.** 1 **8.** 7
9. 10 **10.** 2
Subtraction Number Table:
11 41 61
13 43 63
9 39 59
12 42 62
14 44 64
10 40 60
Count on in sixes:
0 6 12 18 24 30 36 42 48 54 60
66 72 78 84 90 96 102 108 114
SPACE
1. 1, 2, 1, 3.
3. 1, 0, 0.

⏱ **1.** 4 **2.** 20 **3.** 8 **4.** 32 **5.** 10 **6.** 5 **7.** 16
8. 12 **9.** 2 **10.** 36 **11.** 7 **12.** 24 **13.** 14 **14.** 16
15. 12 **16.** 0 **17.** 40 **18.** 8 **19.** 28 **20.** 6
1. 18 **2.** 1 **3.** 7 **4.** 2 **5.** 20 **6.** 8 **7.** 1 **8.** 8 **9.** 2
10. 3 **11.** 12 **12.** 7 **13.** 16 **14.** 9 **15.** 5
16. 0 **17.** 5 **18.** 1 **19.** 4 **20.** 24

MEASUREMENT
1. 15 cm **2.** 16 cm **3.** 17.5 cm **4.** Marcia's
5. Rosa's **6.** 2.5 cm

SPACE
The net will vary according to the box used.

⏱ **1.** 10 **2.** 25 **3.** 60 **4.** 30 **5.** 90 **6.** 35
7. 80 **8.** 40 **9.** 50 **10.** 0 **11.** 40 **12.** 45 **13.** 70
14. 0 **15.** 30 **16.** 0 **17.** 20 **18.** 0
1. 5 **2.** 0 **3.** 80 **4.** 9 **5.** 0 **6.** 3 **7.** 0 **8.** 30 **9.** 2
10. 10 **11.** 0 **12.** 4 **13.** 70 **14.** 5 **15.** 7 **16.** 7
17. 0 **18.** 1

Page 7
Divisions:
1. 18 **2.** 16 **3.** 18 **4.** 24 **5.** 14
Follow the path:
1. 44 **2.** 92 **3.** 29 **4.** 51 **5.** 70 **6.** 45
7. 22 **8.** 21 **9.** 24 **10.** 15

SPACE
1. A square **3.** (a) Go forward 4 steps (b) Turn
left (c) Go forward 4 steps (d) Turn right (e) Go
forward 4 steps (f) Turn left (g) Go forward
4 steps

⏱ **1.** 6 **2.** 8 **3.** 2 **4.** 3 **5.** 5 **6.** 5 **7.** 8 **8.** 11
9. 3 **10.** 6 **11.** 3 **12.** 16 **13.** 6 **14.** 5 **15.** 9
16. 10
1. 10 **2.** 3 **3.** 11 **4.** 1 **5.** 9 **6.** 11 **7.** 10 **8.** 9
9. 14 **10.** 6 **11.** 10 **12.** 2 **13.** 10 **14.** 8 **15.** 12
16. 7

MEASUREMENT
1. Play a game of football — 1 hour
Boil an egg — 3 minutes
Sleep — 8 hours
Read a page — 5 minutes
Hop twice — 2 seconds
Write a letter — 30 minutes
2.

⏱ **1.** 23 **2.** 80 **3.** 46 **4.** 56 **5.** 97 **6.** 40
7. 69 **8.** 50 **9.** 97 **10.** 72 **11.** 90 **12.** 53
13. 63 **14.** 45 **15.** 75
1. 99 **2.** 63 **3.** 74 **4.** 25 **5.** 54 **6.** 46 **7.** 94
8. 74 **9.** 39 **10.** 87 **11.** 58 **12.** 33 **13.** 83
14. 78 **15.** 40

Page 11
1. (a) $1.63 (b) $4.51 (c) $3.80 (d) $1.10
2. $1.10 **3.** $4.51 **4.** (a) 1 $1 coin or 2 50c
coins or 5 20c coins etc.
There are many possible combinations.
(b) 1 50c coin and 1 20c coin and 1 5c coin
or 3 20c coins and 3 5c coins or 3 20c coins
1 10c coin and 1 5c coin.
There are many possible combinations.
5. Prices will vary.

MEASUREMENT

Less than 1 kilogram	About 1 kilogram	More than 1 kilogram
a pair of shoes a pillow	3 plates soap powder 2 litres of milk	a telephone book a brick a school bag

Answers may vary.

UNIT 5
1. (a) 39 cm (b) 24 cm (c) 39 cm (d) 21 cm
2. (a) 15 cm (b) 55 cm, 40 cm
(c) to (e) Answers will vary.
3. (a) Elephants 9.00a.m. Penguins 12.00p.m.
Lions 2.00p.m. Hippopotamus 2.30p.m.
(c) 5½ hours
4. (a) 42 cm (b) 58 cm (c) 1 m or 100 cm.
5. (a) tiger's cage (b) parrot's cage
(c) leopard's cage **6.** $14

UNIT 6
NUMBER Page 14
6 × tables:
6 12 18 24 30 36 42 48 54 60
Number stories:
1. 6 trays **2.** 8 cartons
Count on in 9s:
0 9 18 27 36 45 54 63 72 81 90 99
108 117 126 135 144 153 162 171 180

SPACE
1) 2) 3)
4) 5) 6)

1) rectangle 2) triangle 3) rectangle
4) circle 5) rectangle 6) rectangle

UNIT 7
NUMBER Page 16
9 × table:
9 18 27 36 45 54 63 72 81 90 0
6 × table:
2 4 6 8 1 9 7 3 5 0 10
Doubles:
16 20 40 100 200
8 packets of pegs.
MEASUREMENT
1. B **2.** A **3.** A **4.** B
Time of Day: Answers may vary.
Early morning or late afternoon; midday;
mid-morning or mid-afternoon
If you put the thermometer into hot coffee
the temperature will go up.

UNIT 8
NUMBER Page 18
Across **1.** 57 **2.** 59 **4.** 90 **5.** 67 **7.** 77 **8.** 57
Down **1.** 58 **2.** 50 **3.** 67 **4.** 94 **6.** 75 **7.** 78
9 times:
1 4 6 9 3 7 8 10 5 2

⏱ **1.** 9 **2.** 3 **3.** 2 **4.** 24 **5.** 18 **6.** 9 **7.** 8
8. 5 **9.** 24 **10.** 3 **11.** 27 **12.** 7 **13.** 12
14. 3
1. 82 **2.** 48 **3.** 55 **4.** 42 **5.** 72 **6.** 72 **7.** 20
8. 62 **9.** 71 **10.** 30 **11.** 80 **12.** 83 **13.** 29
14. 73

Page 15
1. 10 hundreds or 100 longs or
1000 shorts
2. 6 hundreds
3. 60 longs
4. 600 shorts
5. 1 thousand and 2 hundreds = 1200
6. 2 thousands, 2 hundreds and
2 tens = 2220
7. 2 thousands, 8 hundreds, 6 tens and
4 ones
8. 4 thousands, 5 hundreds, 7 tens and
9 ones

MEASUREMENT
Answers will vary depending upon
specific items used.

⏱ **1.** 1 **2.** 10 **3.** 12 **4.** 6 **5.** 5 **6.** 7 **7.** 3
8. 8 **9.** 3 **10.** 21 **11.** 3 **12.** 27 **13.** 4 **14.** 3
15. 12 **16.** 3
1. 42 **2.** 30 **3.** 71 **4.** 59 **5.** 32 **6.** 90 **7.** 22
8. 51 **9.** 60 **10.** 70 **11.** 72 **12.** 78 **13.** 43
14. 58 **15.** 70 **16.** 89

Page 17
1. 1 thousand block, 2 hundreds,
3 tens and 7 ones
2. 3 thousand blocks, 5 hundreds,
2 tens and 9 ones
1. 3300 **2.** 2034 **3.** 4006

SPACE
Shapes are all pyramids.
Matching: **1.** Triangular pyramid
2. Rectangular pyramid **3.** Square
pyramid **4.** Pentagonal pyramid
5. Hexagonal pyramid.
Could see a pyramid in **Egypt**.

⏱ **1.** 6 **2.** 24 **3.** 48 **4.** 30 **5.** 60 **6.** 6
7. 12 **8.** 42 **9.** 54 **10.** 0 **11.** 18 **12.** 36
13. 60 **14.** 48 **15.** 24 **16.** 30 **17.** 54
18. 42
1. 64 **2.** 51 **3.** 82 **4.** 100 **5.** 43 **6.** 59
7. 28 **8.** 49 **9.** 81 **10.** 81 **11.** 4 **12.** 90
13. 99 **14.** 42 **15.** 4 **16.** 60 **17.** 50
18. 78

Page 19
1. Two 2. tenths
3. Thirty-hundredths are shaded.
Three-tenths are shaded.
4. Ninety-hundredths are shaded.
Nine-tenths are shaded.
5. Seventy-hundredths are shaded.
Seven-tenths are shaded.
6. Fifty-hundredths are shaded.
Five-tenths are shaded.
Who Am I?   30, 42

UNIT 9
NUMBER   Page 20

1.
```
  7 8
- 5 5
  2 3
```
2.
```
  3 8
- 1 6
  2 2
```
3.
```
  4 4
- 2 3
  2 1
```

Page 21
1. (a) 0.35 (b) 0.75 (c) 0.82 (d) 1.0
(e) 0.45
2. (a) 8 tenths (b) 6 tenths and
1 hundredth (c) 5 tenths (d) 7 tenths
3.

 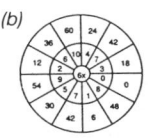 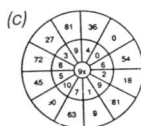

(a)   (b)   (c)

UNIT 10
1. (a) 39 cm (b) Answers will vary.
(c) Answers will vary.
2. (a) 100 (b) 100 (c) 200 (d) 50 (e) 100
3. (a) Mama Baby Papa (b) 38 kg (c),
(d) Answers will vary.
4. (a) triangular pyramid (b) triangular
prism (c) rectangular prism (d) sphere
(e) cube (f) cylinder
5. (a) e; t, u, y (b) 12

6. (a) 40 bricks
(b) 13 23 33 43
11 21 31 41
13 23 33 43
7 17 27 37
9 19 29 39
7. (a) 27 m (b) 54 m (c) 81 m
8. (a) Thursday (b) Tuesday and Friday
(c) Wednesday (d) 21 eggs

UNIT 11
NUMBER   Page 24
1. 6 × 3 = 18 or 3 × 6 = 18; 18 ÷ 3 = 6
or 18 ÷ 6 = 3
2. (a) 15 ÷ 5 = 3 or 15 ÷ 5 = 3 (b) 5
5 × 6 = 30 or 6 × 5 = 30 (c) 24
24 ÷ 6 = 4 or 24 ÷ 4 = 6 (d) 7
3 × 7 = 21 or 7 × 3 = 21 (e) 42
42 ÷ 7 = 6 or 42 ÷ 6 = 7
Page 25
1. 1462 2. 3186 3. 5029 4. 1106
5. 1014
1. 18 2. 4 3. 27 4. 9 5. 3 6. 36 7. 6
8. 3 9. 6 10. 6 11. 9 12. 24

MEASUREMENT
Answers will vary.

SPACE
1. The shortest route is a diagonal and uses
3 squares.
2. The longest route uses all 9 squares.

🕐 1. 36 2. 8 3. 6 4. 9 5. 0 6. 42 7. 4
8. 10 9. 5 10. 6 11. 54 12. 5 13. 48 14. 36
15. 7 16. 6 17. 8 18. 1
1. 71 2. 60 3. 92 4. 49 5. 42 6. 90 7. 61
8. 82 9. 39 10. 63 11. 32 12. 81 13. 59
14. 27 15. 48 16. 57 17. 79 18. 88

MEASUREMENT
Answers will vary.

SPACE
1. Answers will vary.
2. Answers will vary.
3. (a) (g); (b) (h); (c) (e); (d) (f).

🕐 1. 18 2. 36 3. 0 4. 27 5. 9 6. 45
7. 72 8. 54 9. 81 10. 63 11. 81 12. 54
13. 63 14. 72 15. 45 16. 54
1. 28 2. 59 3. 40 4. 19 5. 31 6. 79 7. 90
8. 53 9. 65 10. 58 11. 30 12. 71 13. 82
14. 80 15. 32 16. 46

MEASUREMENT
1. 15 minutes 2. 20 minutes 3. 1 hour
4. 1 hour 30 minutes 5. 1 hour 45 minutes
6. afternoon 7. 6 hours 8. 4 hours 25 minutes

SPACE
1. (a) 12 (b) No 2. (a) 12 (b) 12 (c) No
3. Yes 4. No

UNIT 12
NUMBER   Page 26
1. 3133 (a) 3 (b) 1 (c) 3 (d) 3
2. (a) thousands (b) tens
(c) hundreds (d) ones

Page 27
1. 5251 2. 7900 3. 6004 4. 8109
5. 5460

🕐 1. 81 2. 1 3. 36 4. 2 5. 6 6. 3 7. 2
8. 45 9. 7 10. 0 11. 9 12. 8 13. 5 14. 63
15. 72
1. 56 2. 68 3. 87 4. 49 5. 26 6. 78 7. 29
8. 57 9. 16 10. 42 11. 84 12. 34 13. 61
14. 80 15. 24

Number sentences:
1. 8 3 × 8 = 24 or 8 × 3 = 24
2. 60 60 ÷ 10 = 6 or 60 ÷ 6 = 10
3. 6 36 ÷ 6 = 6
4. 5 5 × 9 = 45 or 9 × 5 = 45
Rounding off:
1. 3700, 5700
2. 680, 1130

UNIT 13
NUMBER   Page 28
1. 37c 2. 10c 3. 4 pears for 50c 4. 60c

Page 29
1. 4600 — blue, 4069 — red
2. 3333 — blue, 3033 — red
3. 7899 — red, 7988 — blue
4. 5050 — red, 5100 — blue
Ordering:
6960 6970 6980 6990
3100 3200 3400 3500
Calculator: 700
Add: 800 90 202

UNIT 14
NUMBER   Page 30
1. 0 8 16 24 32 40 48 56 64 72 80 88
96 104 112 120 128 136 144 152
2. 8 16 24 32 40 48 56 64 72 80
3. 8646, 3329, 7099, 4999
4. 8601, 7960, 6667, 4000

Page 31
2. ⁷/₁₀
4. 4 tenths blue green
5. 9 tenths yellow red
6. (a) 70c (b) 70c (c) 3 tenths
Count on in tens:
7. 3020 3030 3040 3050 3060 3070
in sixes: 4018 4024 4030 4036 4042

MEASUREMENT
1.

Children	Height		
Nick	126 cm	1 m 26 cm	1.26 m
Jane	110 cm	1 m 10 cm	1.10 m
Ivan	131 cm	1 m 31 cm	1.31 m
George	115 cm	1 m 15 cm	1.15 m
Lee	169 cm	1 m 69 cm	1.69 m
Maria	122 cm	1 m 22 cm	1.22 m

2. (a) Lee (b) Jane (c) 38 cm (d) 33 cm (e) Jane and Lee 22 cm

UNIT 15
Ring 1:
1. 24 2. 12 3. 0.3 m or 30 cm 4. triangle
4 + 3 + 2 + 1 = 10
Patterns: 1, 5, 9, 13, 17, 21, 25, 29,
33 (adding 4)
2, 7, 12, 17, 22, 27, 32, 37, 42 (adding 5)
Ring 2:
1. $1.40 2. $2.40 3. $2.60
Tickets 1. $10 2. 2 adult and 1 child
Patterns:

UNIT 16
NUMBER   Page 34
1. 50 km 2. 77 km 3. 59 km 4. 74 km

MEASUREMENT
Answers will vary.

SPACE
1. (c), 2. (b), 3. (a), 4. (d)

🕐 1. 48 2. 30 3. 9 4. 8 5. 42 6. 3
7. 6 8. 9 9. 5 10. 15 11. 24 12. 6 13. 8
14. 5 15. 9 16. 9
1. 57 2. 88 3. 40 4. 77 5. 49 6. 68 7. 30
8. 61 9. 18 10. 37 11. 26 12. 65 13. 34
14. 67 15. 87 16. 55

MEASUREMENT
Answers will vary.

SPACE
1. Library 2. Office 3. Turn right at the
library door, Walk 7 steps, Turn right,
Walk 4 steps.

🕐 1. 48 2. 90 3. 9 4. 9 5. 42 6. 9
7. 8 8. 6 9. 5 10. 45 11. 24 12. 4 13. 8
14. 1 15. 9 16. 27 17. 0
1. 75 2. 44 3. 9 4. 62 5. 40 6. 73 7. 30
8. 72 9. 93 10. 51 11. 76 12. 29 13. 59
14. 76 15. 37 16. 88 17. 35

SPACE
1. Yes
2. Patterns will vary.
3. Answers will vary.

Ring 3:
1. 11.00 2. 12.00 3. 2.30 4. 3½ hours
5. Clowns 6. Trapeze 7. 30 minutes, 30
minutes
Patterns: 1, 2, 4, 7, 11, 16, 22, 29, 37,
46 (adding 0, then 1, then 2 etc.)
Ring 4:
1. 20 2. 10 3. 15 4. 45 5. No
6. The families would be of different sizes.

🕐 1. 18 2. 8 3. 7 4. 9 5. 16 6. 6 7. 36
8. 9 9. 7 10. 7 11. 8 12. 8 13. 6 14. 10
1. 16 2. 69 3. 86 4. 37 5. 75 6. 58 7. 29

Page 35
1. 50 **hundredths**
one **half**
2. 8 × 2 = 16   8 × 9 = 72   8 × 10 = 80
8 × 5 = 40   8 × 1 = 8
8 × 6 = 48   8 × 8 = 64   8 × 4 = 32
8 × 7 = 56   8 × 3 = 24
3. (a) 10 cm (b) 20 cm (c) 50 cm
(d) 8 (e) 80 cm
4. (a) 10 mL (b) 20 mL (c) 50 mL
(d) 8 (e) 80 mL

SPACE

8. 48 **9.** 65 **10.** 29 **11.** 57 **12.** 78 **13.** 86
14. 97

MEASUREMENT

1. 11.54 a.m., 12.06 p.m.
2. 4 minutes, 7 minutes, 9 minutes
3. 12.14 p.m., 12.17 p.m., 12.23 p.m.
4. Circular Quay and St James. It takes the least
amount of time to travel from one to the other.

UNIT 17

NUMBER   Page 36
1. 36 km **2.** 36 km **3.** 35 km **4.** 39 km
6 times:
1. 36 **2.** 3 **3.** 3 **4.** 5 **5.** 8 **6.** 4 **7.** 60
8. 7 **9.** 54 **10.** 8 **11.** 7 **12.** 2 **13.** 5
14. 10 **15.** 2 **16.** 9 **17.** 4 **18.** 6 **19.** 1

Page 37
7 14 21 28 35 42 49 56 63 70
1) 25 blue **2)** 18 green **3)** 29 red
4) 48 pink **5)** 82 brown

1. 4 **2.** 40 **3.** 9 **4.** 80 **5.** 96 **6.** 5 **7.** 7 **8.** 90
9. 10 **10.** 5 **11.** 8 **12.** 10 **13.** 8 **14.** 40 **15.** 5
16. 10 **17.** 50 **18.** 5
1. 43 **2.** 63 **3.** 82 **4.** 30 **5.** 82 **6.** 63 **7.** 71 **8.** 54
9. 81 **10.** 61 **11.** 92 **12.** 62 **13.** 51 **14.** 64
15. 34 **16.** 78 **17.** 42 **18.** 73

MEASUREMENT
Answers will vary.

SPACE
1. Handball **2.** Soccer

UNIT 18

NUMBER   Page 38
1. 9 **2.** 8 **3.** 6 **4.** 6 **5.** 27 **6.** 4 **7.** 8 **8.** 5
9. 2 **10.** 10 **11.** 7 **12.** 3 **13.** 4 **14.** 9
15. 27 **16.** 9 **17.** 5
Rounding off:
1. (a) 70 (b) 50 (d) 890 (d) 640 (e) 300
2. (a) 400 (b) 800 (c) 6300 (d) 3900
(e) 3000

Page 39
1. (a) 0.2 (b) 0.08 (c) 0.16 (d) 0.83
2. (a) 0.1 (b) 0.3 (c) 0.09
3. (a) 22 (b) 32 (c) 44 (d) 34
7 × table
1   4
7   6
2   3
5   9
7   10

1. 27 **2.** 2 **3.** 3 **4.** 9 **5.** 6 **6.** 1 **7.** 6 **8.** 5
9. 15 **10.** 7 **11.** 7 **12.** 3 **13.** 12 **14.** 9 **15.** 4
16. 10 **17.** 3
1. 15 **2.** 45 **3.** 86 **4.** 59 **5.** 36 **6.** 89 **7.** 37 **8.** 57
9. 40 **10.** 59 **11.** 68 **12.** 79 **13.** 30 **14.** 47
15. 68 **16.** 18 **17.** 66

MEASUREMENT
1. 300 mL **2.** 100 mL **3.** 400 mL

SPACE
1. (a) cup (b) telephone pole
2. (a) triangular prism (b) triangular pyramid
(c) sphere
3. Answers will vary.

UNIT 19

NUMBER   Page 40
1. 32 **2.** 56 **3.** 40 **4.** 72 **5.** 80
6. 48 **7.** 64 **8.** 9 **9.** 16 **10.** 0 **11.** 72
12. 56 **13.** 64 **14.** 48 **15.** 6 **16.** 4 **17.** 9
18. 7 **19.** 8 **20.** 5
1. 42 **2.** 98 **3.** 35 **4.** 63 **5.** 71 **6.** 54
7. 85 **8.** 64 **9.** 32 **10.** 53 **11.** 66 **12.** 52
13. 85 **14.** 41 **15.** 74 **16.** 30 **17.** 43
18. 65 **19.** 86 **20.** 54

Page 41
Money: **1.** $25 **2.** $30 **3.** $120
Place-value chart:
1. (f) **2.** (e) **3.** (c) **4.** (d) **5.** (b) **6.** (a)
1. 10 **2.** 9 **3.** 8 **4.** 4 **5.** 3 **6.** 5 **7.** 7 **8.** 9 **9.** 6 **10.** 4
11. 7 **12.** 5 **13.** 6 **14.** 8 **15.** 9 **16.** 9

MEASUREMENT
Answers will vary.

SPACE
Answers will vary.

UNIT 20

Cutting cakes:
1. ▭ **2.** ▭ ○ **3.** ○ ◠

Plant prices:
1. (a) $11.50 (b) $28 (c) $7.99
2. Hexagon
3. (a) 3.20 (b) 7.00 (c) 9.40 (d) 1.40
4. (a) $40.20 (b) $110 (c) $190 (d) $395

Page 43
1. (a) 130 (b) 20 (c) 30 (d) 30
2. (a) $86.90 (b) $150.50 (c) $649.50
(d) $605.95
3. (a) 54c (b) $28 (c) 45c (d) $50 (e) $5
(f) $10.48
4. (a) $20 (b) $13 (c) $45
5. (a) 24 (b) 36 (c) 35.

UNIT 21

NUMBER   Page 44
Calculator: 0.7
Add: 0.6, 0.47, 0.9, 0.43

Page 45
Arrays will vary.
Squared numbers: **1.** 1 **2.** 4 **3.** 9
Factors: **1.** 8 **2.** 12 **3.** 1, 2, 3, 4, 6, 9, 12,
18, 36 **4.** 1, 2, 3, 6, 9, 18

SPACE
1. (a), (b) **2.** (c), (e) **3.** (d), (f) **4.** [shapes] **5.** [shapes]

 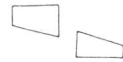
1. 32 **2.** 48 **3.** 8 **4.** 40 **5.** 24
6. 16 **7.** 56 **8.** 80 **9.** 64 **10.** 72 **11.** 8
12. 7 **13.** 9 **14.** 6
1. 34 **2.** 56 **3.** 88 **4.** 29 **5.** 55 **6.** 75
7. 77 **8.** 39 **9.** 16 **10.** 53 **11.** 48
12. 63 **13.** 67 **14.** 40

MEASUREMENT
Answers will vary.

UNIT 22

NUMBER   Page 46
Notes may vary. Fewest are shown.
1. | $50 | $10 | $5 |
2. | $100 | $20 | $5 |
3. | $100 | $100 | $20 | $10 | $5 |
4. | $100 | $10 | $5 |

Page 47
1. 16 **2.** 25 **3.** 36 **4.** 9, 18, 27, 36, 45, 54, 63,
72, 81, 90, 99, 108 **5.** 15 **6.** 25
7. 12 (or its multiples)
8. 36 (or its multiples)
9. 18 (or its multiples)

SPACE
1 face visible; 11, 2 faces visible; 6, 3 faces
visible; 1.
View of objects: Answers may vary.

1. 28 **2.** 49 **3.** 35 **4.** 14 **5.** 63
6. 21 **7.** 7 **8.** 42 **9.** 56 **10.** 70 **11.** 7
12. 5 **13.** 8 **14.** 6 **15.** 9 **16.** 4
1. 60 **2.** 80 **3.** 72 **4.** 42 **5.** 64 **6.** 91
7. 36 **8.** 73 **9.** 93 **10.** 35 **11.** 55
12. 67 **13.** 86 **14.** 44 **15.** 51 **16.** 57

MEASUREMENT
1. (a) 5.20 a.m. (b) 1.00 p.m. (c)
5.00 p.m. (d) 3.00 a.m. (e) 12.06 p.m.
(f) 1.00 a.m.
2. 5.35 a.m., 6.20 a.m., 8.00 a.m.,
5.25 p.m., 6.00 p.m.
3. (a) 12.15 p.m. (b) 7.05 p.m.
(c) 12.52 a.m.
4. (a) afternoon (b) morning
(c) afternoon
5. (a) 4.15 a.m. (b) 1.00 p.m.
(c) 10.35 p.m.

UNIT 23

NUMBER   Page 48
1. 12 **2.** 3 cups **3.** 18 **4.** 20 km

Page 49
1. 72 **2.** 111 **3.** 78 **4.** 84 **5.** 80 **6.** 85 **7.** 85
8. 93
Rounding off:
1. 7000 **2.** 3000 **3.** 5000 **4.** 8000

MEASUREMENT
1. 2 m **2.** 2 m **3.** 0.7 m **4.** 1 m **5.** 1.3 m
6. Answers will vary.

1. 0 **2.** 35 **3.** 21 **4.** 42 **5.** 7
6. 70 **7.** 49 **8.** 14 **9.** 56 **10.** 63 **11.** 28
12. 2 **13.** 11 **14.** 6 **15.** 4 **16.** 7 **17.** 8
1. 34 **2.** 29 **3.** 55 **4.** 36 **5.** 77 **6.** 44
7. 67 **8.** 33 **9.** 52 **10.** 78 **11.** 65
12. 83 **13.** 22 **14.** 16 **15.** 38 **16.** 24
17. 71

SPACE

	Yellow	Pink	Green
△	△		△
○	○	○	○
□		□	

UNIT 24

NUMBER   Page 50
1. (a) 4250 mL, 4.25 L (b) 136 cm, 1.36 m
(c) 1 whole and 47 hundredths, 1.47
(d) 8 m 42 cm, 8.42 m (e) 550 cm, 5.5 m
(f) 6 tenths, 0.6 (g) 2 litres and 80 mL, 2.08 L

Page 51
1. 18 **2.** 36 **3.** 13 **4.** 23 **5.** 18 **6.** 56
What goes up but never comes down?
1. 55 **2.** 65 **3.** 46 **4.** 51 **5.** 32 **6.** 37 **7.** 17
YOUR AGE!

SPACE

Side View   Top View   Sides visible:

Side View [bottle]   Top View ◎

Side View   Top View

1. 48 **2.** 6 **3.** 60 **4.** 18 **5.** 8 **6.** 3
7. 54 **8.** 9 **9.** 42 **10.** 6 **11.** 6 **12.** 7
13. 30 **14.** 6 **15.** 24
1. 44 **2.** 93 **3.** 45 **4.** 87 **5.** 94 **6.** 65
7. 36 **8.** 54 **9.** 96 **10.** 33 **11.** 65
12. 75 **13.** 97 **14.** 62 **15.** 58

MEASUREMENT
2 × 500g, 5 × 200g, 10 × 100g
Mass of each object: 700g, 900g,
300g
Total mass: 1800g   900g
more than 1kg.

3	2	1	0
3	3	1	
1	4	5	2
1	5	8	4
1	5	5	1

UNIT 25
1. West 5 paces, north 10, west 13, south 6, east 4.
2. (a) 15.9 m (b) 4.85 m (c) 5.5 m (d) 1.2 m
3. (a) 8404 (b) 6999 (c) 4790
4. (a) $45 (b) $700 (c) $300 (d) $90 (e) $1135
5. 7 July
6. 27 July

UNIT 26
NUMBER   Page 54
1. 4 and 8 (or any other multiples of 4)
2. 8, 16, 24
3. 1, 2, 3, 5, 6, 10, 15, 30
4. 18
5. 1, 2, 3, 4, 6, 8, 12, 16, 24, 48
6. 6, 12, 18, 24
7. Any 3 from 1 2, 4, 8, 16
8. 25 It is not a multiple of 8.
9. 48

MEASUREMENT
Answers will vary.
More likely capacity:
250 mL, 400 mL, 5 mL, 20 L

SPACE
2.
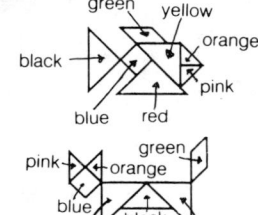

3. Missing shape is black.

UNIT 27
NUMBER   Page 56
1. 8 for each, 1 left over 2. 6 for each, 1 left over 3. 5 to each cage, 2 left over

Page 57
Across 1. 899 3. 417 5. 600 6. 30
7. 491 8. 48 9. 82 10. 4650 11. 42
12. 9800 13. 37
Down 1. 87 2. 9001 3. 45 4. 100
5. 692 6. 385 7. 48 8. 46 10. 420
11. 40
1. 7000 2. 6800 3. 7000 4. 3700
5. 6900
Multiplication 1. 81 2. 48 3. 42 4. 36
5. 36 6. 56 7. 54 8. 72 9. 45

UNIT 28
NUMBER   Page 58
1. 6 r 1 2. 7 r 1 3. 5 r 1 4. 6 r 2 5. 4 r 5
6. 6 r 6 7. 42 8. 69 9. 64
Decimals:
1. One and nine-tenths
2. Six tenths
3. Three and seventy-one hundredths
4. Thirty-eight hundredths
5. Six and six-hundredths

MEASUREMENT
1. 2 cm² 2. 3.5 cm² 3. 2 cm² 4. 2 cm²
5. 8 cm² 6. 4 cm²
1. Perimeter, 12 cm; Area, 6 cm²

Page 53
36, 24, 54, 64, 24, 53, 42
56, 36, 24, 48, 39, 24, 36, 32
CAPTAIN SCARFACE
Number problems:
1. 8 2. 162 3. 9½ 4. 69
Designs of flags will vary.

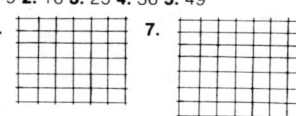 1. 2 2. 1 3. 9 4. 8 5. 1 6. 9 7. 36 8. 9
9. 54 10. 7 11. 5 12. 63 13. 81 14. 54
15. 8 16. 5 17. 7 18. 3
1. 22 2. 45 3. 75 4. 61 5. 47 6. 66 7. 43 8. 84
9. 65 10. 88 11. 14 12. 63 13. 35 14. 54
15. 36 16. 77 17. 62 18. 76

Page 55
1. 9 2. 16 3. 25 4. 36 5. 49

6. 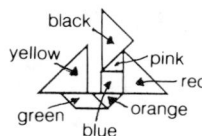   7.

1. (a) 1300 (b) 2600 (c) 7000 (d) 7800
(e) 4000
2. (a) Four thousand three hundred
(b) Five thousand and sixty
1. 2, 6, 11, 9, 3, 6, 10, 2
2. 4, 16, 8, 24, 4, 9, 36, 42
3. 5, 30, 10, 18, 2, 12, 3, 15, 5

1. 4 2. 8 3. 8 4. 6 5. 40 6. 7 7. 7 8. 9
9. 8 10. 64 11. 8 12. 4 13. 3 14. 8 15. 7
1. 18 2. 49 3. 45 4. 72 5. 54 6. 42 7. 40
8. 63 9. 35 10. 36 11. 64 12. 32 13. 30
14. 56 15. 36

MEASUREMENT
1. yellow 2. D 3. A 4. green 5. red, E
6. white, A 7. Answers will vary.

SPACE
Shape when open paper is a square.
It is called a **rhombus**.
You have made a **square**.

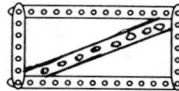 1. 7 2. 63 3. 2 4. 7 5. 6 6. 5 7. 8 8. 21
9. 7 10. 4 11. 49 12. 21 13. 28 14. 63
15. 5 16. 10
1. 63 2. 64 3. 81 4. 48 5. 54 6. 56 7. 40
8. 72 9. 36 10. 49 11. 45 12. 30 13. 42
14. 54 15. 28 16. 72

Page 59
Larger:
1. 0.9 2. 0.89 3. 0.43 4. 1.3 5. 1.0
Change:
1. $2 2. $3.50 3. $4.20 4. $0.50 5. $4.90
Errors:
5 × 1 = 5 not 0, 2 × 2 = 4 not 3, 4 × 2 = 8 not 9,
8 × 2 = 16 not 17, 6 × 3 = 18 not 19, 1 × 4 = 4

Page 53 (continued)
2. Perimeter, 16 cm; Area, 12 cm²

SPACE
2. (a) Top shelf, first from right
(b) Middle shelf, third from right

UNIT 29
NUMBER   Page 60
1. 4, 6, 18, 12, 22, 20, 4, 12, 21, 3, 21, 12
2. 7, 14, 20, 2, 4, 14, 7, 21, 42, 40, 8, 4
3. 5, 6, 30, 20, 5, 10, 15, 5, 15, 21, 18

Page 61
Calculator Targets — answers may vary.
1. (a) 6 ÷ 6 + 6 = (b) 6 ÷ 6 + 6 + 6 =
2. (a) 5 + 5 ÷ 5 + 5 + 5 = (b) 11
(c) 5 + 5 + 5 + 5 × 5 - 5 - 5 - 5 ÷ 5 =

SPACE
1. Answers will vary.
2. (a) b and c
(b)

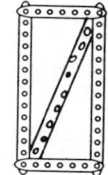

UNIT 30
1. $404 2. $33 3. (a) $4206 (b) 4620 (c) $4606
4. (a) 55 mins (b) 1 hr 5 mins (c) 1 hr 35 mins
(d) 2 hrs 40 mins
6. $1860, $5099, $5900, $1999

not 0, 5 × 4 = 20 not 22, 7 × 5 = 35 not 36,
10 × 5 = 50 not 55, 5 × 6 = 30 not 36, 3 × 7
= 21 not 20, 8 × 7 = 56 not 54, 5 × 9 = 45
not 46, 9 × 9 = 81 not 82, 2 × 10 = 20 not 22

1. 8 2. 9 3. 0 4. 10 5. 7 6. 9 7. 9
8. 6 9. 4 10. 6 11. 5 12. 8 13. 6 14. 7
15. 1 16. 7
1. 10 2. 11 3. 16 4. 8 5. 4 6. 10 7. 9
8. 10 9. 12 10. 13 11. 15 12. 12 13. 7
14. 8 15. 10 16. 8

MEASUREMENT
Twelve months:
January 31, February 28, March 31,
April 30, May 31, June 30, July 31,
August 31, September 30, October 31,
November 30, December 31
Days of week:
Sunday, Monday, Tuesday, Wednesday,
Thursday, Friday, Saturday
60 secs, 60 mins, 24 hrs, 7 days,
2 weeks, 10 decades, 100 years
Order:
second, minute, hour, day, week,
fortnight, decade, century

Page 63
1. (a) $63 (b) $17 (c) $8 (d) $18 (e) $2
(f) $54 (g) $6 (h) $14
3. (a) 87 kg (b) $36

11.00	Opening Parade
11.30	Acrobats
12.00	Lion Taming
12.45	Clowns
1.00	Trapeze
2.00	Horses
2.30	Close

Ring 3

1. What time is the opening parade?

2. When is the lion taming?

3. What time does the circus performance finish?

4. How long is the whole show?

5. Which is the shortest act?

6. Which is the longest act?

7. For how long do the horses perform?

   the acrobats?

Ring 4

Look at the chart for the tickets sold on Monday.

1. How many tickets were sold to children?

2. How many were sold to adults?

3. How many were sold to families?

4. How many tickets were sold altogether?

5. Can you use this chart to figure out how many people were at the circus on Monday?

6. Why or why not? _____

   _____

   _____

			20
			15
			10
			5
Child	Adult	Family	

Tickets sold Monday

NUMBER

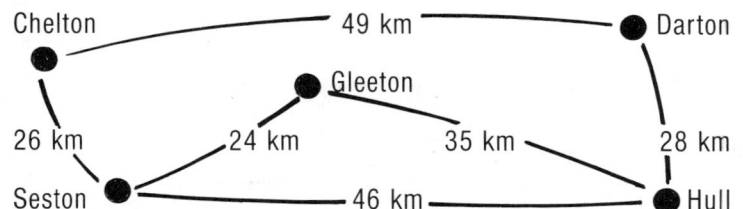

Chelton ———— 49 km ———— Darton

Gleeton

26 km   24 km   35 km   28 km

Seston ———— 46 km ———— Hull

Use the map to work out the distances between these towns.

1. Chelton, Seston and Gleeton

2. Chelton, Darton and Hull

3. Hull, Gleeton and Seston

4. Seston, Hull and Darton

1. 2 x 9 = ☐
2. 16 ÷ 2 = ☐
3. 4 x ☐ = 28
4. 36 ÷ 4 = ☐
5. 8 x 2 = ☐
6. 24 ÷ 4 = ☐
7. 4 x 9 = ☐
8. 18 ÷ 2 = ☐
9. 2 x ☐ = 14
10. 28 ÷ 4 = ☐
11. 4 x ☐ = 32
12. 32 ÷ 4 = ☐
13. 2 x ☐ = 12
14. 20 ÷ 2 = ☐

1. 21 – 5 = ☐
2. 74 – 5 = ☐
3. 91 – 5 = ☐
4. 42 – 5 = ☐
5. 80 – 5 = ☐
6. 63 – 5 = ☐
7. 34 – 5 = ☐
8. 53 – 5 = ☐
9. ☐ – 5 = 60
10. ☐ – 5 = 24
11. ☐ – 5 = 52
12. ☐ – 5 = 73
13. ☐ – 5 = 81
14. ☐ – 5 = 92

MEASUREMENT

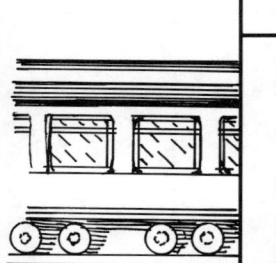

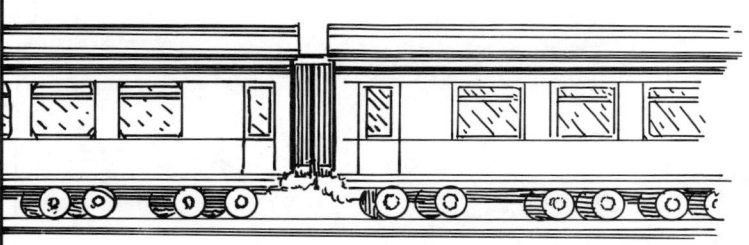

TRAIN TIMETABLE	
Central	11.50 a.m.
Town Hall	11.54 a.m.
Wynyard	11.57 a.m.
Circular Quay	12.01 p.m.
St James	12.03 p.m.
Museum	12.06 p.m.

1. What time does the train arrive at:

Town Hall Station? _____

Museum Station? _____

2. How long does it take to travel from:

Central to Town Hall? _____

Central to Wynyard? _____

Town Hall to St James? _____

3. If the train is 20 minutes late, what time would it arrive at:

Town Hall? _____

Wynyard? _____

St James? _____

4. Which stations do you think might be the closest?

_____ and _____

Why? _____

1. Colour five-tenths.

This is [   ] hundredths

or one [   ]

2.
8 x [ ] = 16   8 x [ ] = 72   8 x [ ] = 80
8 x [ ] = 40   8 x [ ] = 8
8 x [ ] = 48   8 x [ ] = 64   8 x [ ] = 32
8 x [ ] = 56   8 x [ ] = 24

0   20cm   40cm   60cm   80cm   1m

3. (a) Colour one-tenth red. How many cm? [   ]

(b) Colour two-tenths yellow. How many cm is this? [   ]

(c) Colour five-tenths blue. How many cm is this? [   ]

(d) How many tenths are coloured? [   ]

(e) How many cm is this? [   ]

80mL
60mL
40mL
20mL

4. (a) Colour one-tenth blue. How many mL? [   ]

(b) Colour two-tenths red. How many mL? [   ]

(c) Colour five-tenths yellow. How many mL is this? [   ]

(d) How many tenths are coloured? [   ]

(e) How many mL is this? [   ]

S P A C E

Draw the shape you would get if you turned each shape on its side and slid it along. Then turn it again.

Make a pattern by drawing the shape you get when you flip and then slide each shape along. The first one is done for you.

Now make a pattern of your own by flipping, sliding and turning.

UNIT 17
▲▲▲▲▲▲

1. Grafton is 65 km away. We have travelled 29 km. How far have we got to go? ☐

2. Glen Innes is 81 km away. We have travelled 45 km. How far have we got to go? ☐

3. Muswellbrook is 73 km away. We have travelled 38 km. How far have we got to go? ☐

4. Tamworth is 66 km away. We have travelled 27 km. How far have we got to go? ☐

Complete these.

1. $6 \times 6 =$ ☐
2. $18 \div 6 =$ ☐
3. $6 \times$ ☐ $= 18$
4. $30 \div 6 =$ ☐
5. $6 \times$ ☐ $= 48$
6. $24 \div 6 =$ ☐
7. $6 \times 10 =$ ☐
8. $42 \div 6 =$ ☐
9. $6 \times 9 =$ ☐
10. $48 \div 6 =$ ☐
11. $6 \times$ ☐ $= 42$
12. $12 \div 6 =$ ☐
13. $6 \times$ ☐ $= 30$
14. $60 \div 6 =$ ☐
15. ☐ $\times 6 = 12$
16. $54 \div 6 =$ ☐
17. $6 \times$ ☐ $= 24$
18. $36 \div 6 =$ ☐
19. ☐ $\times 6 = 6$

1. $40 \div 10 =$ ☐
2. $5 \times 8 =$ ☐
3. $45 \div 5 =$ ☐
4. $10 \times 8 =$ ☐
5. $90 \div 10 =$ ☐
6. $6 \times$ ☐ $= 30$
7. $35 \div 5 =$ ☐
8. $9 \times 10 =$ ☐
9. $70 \div$ ☐ $= 7$
10. $9 \times$ ☐ $= 45$
11. $40 \div 5 =$ ☐
12. $7 \times$ ☐ $= 70$
13. $80 \div 10 =$ ☐
14. $8 \times 5 =$ ☐
15. $25 \div 5 =$ ☐
16. ☐ $\times 6 = 60$
17. ☐ $\div 10 = 5$
18. $7 \times$ ☐ $= 35$

1. $38 + 5 =$ ☐
2. $60 + 3 =$ ☐
3. $78 + 4 =$ ☐
4. $27 + 3 =$ ☐
5. $77 + 5 =$ ☐
6. $59 + 4 =$ ☐
7. $67 + 4 =$ ☐
8. $49 + 5 =$ ☐
9. $78 + 3 =$ ☐
10. $56 + 5 =$ ☐
11. $89 + 3 =$ ☐
12. $58 + 4 =$ ☐
13. $48 + 3 =$ ☐
14. $61 + 3 =$ ☐
15. $29 + 5 =$ ☐
16. $74 + 4 =$ ☐
17. $38 + 4 =$ ☐
18. $68 + 5 =$ ☐

▲▲

Look in your kitchen cupboard. Write down items in the correct column in this chart:

Less than 200 g	Between 200 g and 500 g	Between 500 g and 1 kg	More than 1 kg

1	2	3	4	5	6	7	8	9	10
11	12	13	14	15	16	17	18	19	20
21	22	23	24	25	26	27	28	29	30
31	32	33	34	35	36	37	38	39	40
41	42	43	44	45	46	47	48	49	50
51	52	53	54	55	56	57	58	59	60
61	62	63	64	65	66	67	68	69	70
71	72	73	74	75	76	77	78	79	80
81	82	83	84	85	86	87	88	89	90
91	92	93	94	95	96	97	98	99	100

Use a yellow pencil to colour in 7.
Count 7 more and colour the square yellow.
Keep counting 7 more and colouring in the number yellow each time.

Use the grid to complete these.

7 x 1 = ☐   7 x 2 = ☐   7 x 3 = ☐
7 x 4 = ☐   7 x 5 = ☐   7 x 6 = ☐
7 x 7 = ☐   7 x 8 = ☐   7 x 9 = ☐
                    7 x 10 = ☐

Colour on the grid:

1. Half of 50, blue.
2. The nearest even number more than 16, green.
3. 40 – 11 =, red.
4. Double 24, pink.
5. The total of 23, 41 and 18, brown.

▲▲▲

S P A C E

Eric made a column graph of the class's favourite playground games.

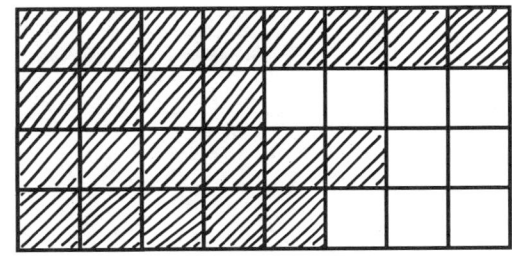

Handball
Soccer
Elastics
Skipping

1. Which game was the most popular?

_____

2. Which was the least popular?

_____

3. Use the grid on the right to redraw this column graph vertically.

4. Find out the most popular games for your class.

NUMBER

Complete these.

1. 9 x ☐ = 81
2. 72 ÷ 9 = ☐
3. 9 x ☐ = 54
4. 54 ÷ 9 = ☐
5. 3 x 9 = ☐
6. 36 ÷ 9 = ☐
7. 9 x ☐ = 72
8. 45 ÷ 9 = ☐
9. 9 x ☐ = 18
10. 90 ÷ 9 = ☐
11. ☐ x 9 = 63
12. 27 ÷ 9 = ☐
13. 9 x ☐ = 36
14. 63 ÷ 7 = ☐
15. 9 x 3 = ☐
16. 81 ÷ 9 = ☐
17. 9 x ☐ = 45

1. Round off to the nearest ten:

(a) 66 _____

(b) 52 _____

(c) 891 _____

(d) 638 _____

(e) 298 _____

2. Round off to the nearest hundred:

(a) 364 _____

(b) 827 _____

(c) 6291 _____

(d) 3856 _____

(e) 2961 _____

1. 3 x 9 = ☐
2. 6 ÷ 3 = ☐
3. 8 x ☐ = 24
4. 27 ÷ 3 = ☐
5. 18 ÷ 3 = ☐
6. 3 x ☐ = 3
7. 3 x ☐ = 18
8. 15 ÷ 3 = ☐
9. 3 x 5 = ☐
10. 3 x ☐ = 21
11. 21 ÷ 3 = ☐
12. 30 ÷ ☐ = 10
13. 3 x 4 = ☐
14. 3 x ☐ = 27
15. 12 ÷ 3 = ☐
16. 3 x ☐ = 30
17. 9 ÷ 3 = ☐

1. 20 - 5 = ☐
2. 48 - 3 = ☐
3. 90 - 4 = ☐
4. 63 - 4 = ☐
5. 41 - 5 = ☐
6. 92 - 3 = ☐
7. 40 - 3 = ☐
8. 62 - 5 = ☐
9. 44 - 4 = ☐
10. 62 - 3 = ☐
11. 72 - 4 = ☐
12. 84 - 5 = ☐
13. 33 - 3 = ☐
14. 51 - 4 = ☐
15. 73 - 5 = ☐
16. 21 - 3 = ☐
17. 70 - 4 = ☐

MEASUREMENT

Nancy measured the volume of some rocks. What was the volume of each rock?

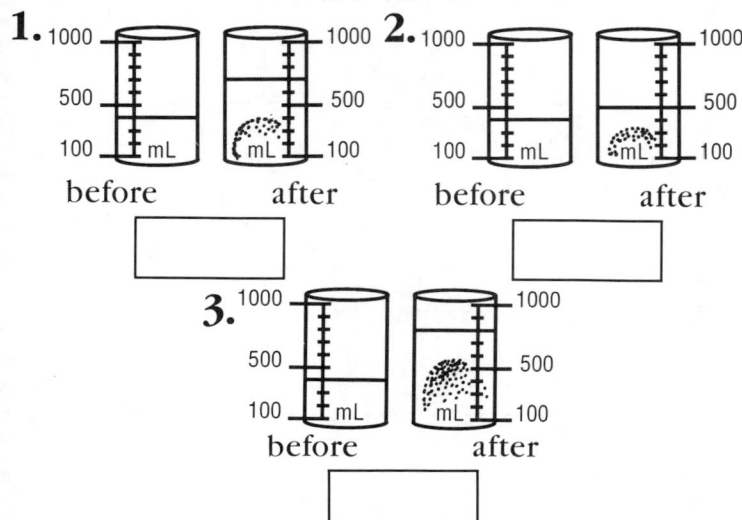

Use a measuring container like this or make your own: measure in 100 mL and make a mark. Keep doing this until you measure to 1000 mL.

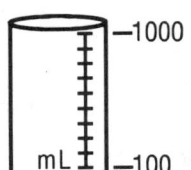

Use this container to find the volume of 4 items in your classroom or home (to the nearest 100mL).

Object	Estimate	Measured

1. Write as a decimal:

(a)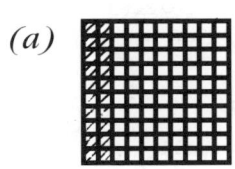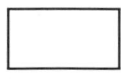

(c)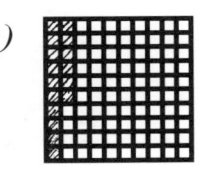

(b)  ☐

(d) ☐ ☐

Complete these.

☐ x 7 = 7   7 x ☐ = 28

☐ x 7 = 49   7 x ☐ = 42

7 x ☐ = 14   7 x ☐ = 21

7 x ☐ = 35   7 x ☐ = 63

7 x ☐ = 49   7 x ☐ = 70

2. Show the decimal on the grid.

(a) 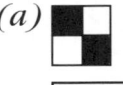 0·1   *(b)* 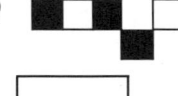 0·3   *(c)* 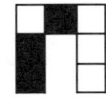 0·09

3. A black square is worth ten. A white square is worth one. What are these diagrams worth?

(a)  ☐   *(b)*  ☐   *(c)* ☐   *(d)*  ☐

SPACE

1. Can you name the object?

(a) Top view   and   Side view   ☐

(b) Top view   and   Side view   ☐

2. Can you name these 3D solids?

(a) _____

(b) _____

(c) _____

3. Choose an object and draw the views. Name: _____

Top View	Side View	Bottom View

NUMBER

Find out who the people are on:

1. the [$5] note
(a) _____
(b) _____

2. the [$10] note
(a) _____
(b) _____

3. the [$50] note
(a) _____
(b) _____

4. the [$100] note
(a) _____
(b) _____

1. $4 \times 8 = \square$
2. $8 \times 7 = \square$
3. $5 \times 8 = \square$
4. $9 \times 8 = \square$
5. $8 \times 10 = \square$
6. $6 \times 8 = \square$
7. $8 \times 8 = \square$
8. $1 \times 8 = \square$
9. $8 \times 2 = \square$
10. $0 \times 8 = \square$
11. $9 \times 8 = \square$
12. $7 \times 8 = \square$
13. $8 \times 8 = \square$
14. $6 \times 8 = \square$
15. $\square \times 8 = 48$
16. $\square \times 8 = 32$
17. $8 \times \square = 72$
18. $8 \times \square = 56$
19. $8 \times \square = 64$
20. $8 \times \square = 40$

1. $36 + 6 = \square$
2. $92 + 6 = \square$
3. $29 + 6 = \square$
4. $57 + 6 = \square$
5. $65 + 6 = \square$
6. $48 + 6 = \square$
7. $79 + 6 = \square$
8. $58 + 6 = \square$
9. $26 + 6 = \square$
10. $47 + 6 = \square$
11. $59 + 7 = \square$
12. $45 + 7 = \square$
13. $78 + 7 = \square$
14. $34 + 7 = \square$
15. $67 + 7 = \square$
16. $23 + 7 = \square$
17. $36 + 7 = \square$
18. $58 + 7 = \square$
19. $79 + 7 = \square$
20. $47 + 7 = \square$

MEASUREMENT

To find the circumference you can measure around an object using a piece of string or streamer.

You can also roll it along the string.

Use the methods to measure the circumference of these objects.

Circumference	Jam lid	Can of food	Toy wheel	Bicycle wheel
Using string or a streamer around the object				
By rolling the object and marking 1 revolution on the string				

Write a sentence about one of the people on the dollar notes explaining why he/she is there.

_____

_____

_____

Draw lines to match the numbers to the place-value chart.

	Ones	· Tenths	Hundredths	
1.	0	▯▯	▦	*(a)* 1·04
2.	▦	▯▯▯▯▯	▫	*(b)* 2·25
3.	▦	▯▯▯	▦	*(c)* 1·36
4.	0	▯▯▯▯▯▯	0	*(d)* 0·60
5.	▦ ▦	▯▯	▦	*(e)* 1·52
6.	▦	0	▯	*(f)* 0·28

How much money?

1.

[   ]

2.

[   ]

3. $5 $100 $10 $5

[   ]

1. $6 \times \square = 60$ **9.** $9 \times \square = 54$

2. $54 \div 6 = \square$ **10.** $24 \div 6 = \square$

3. $9 \times \square = 72$ **11.** $6 \times \square = 42$

4. $36 \div 9 = \square$ **12.** $45 \div 9 = \square$

5. $18 \div 6 = \square$ **13.** $6 \times \square = 36$

6. $9 \times \square = 45$ **14.** $48 \div 6 = \square$

7. $63 \div 9 = \square$ **15.** $3 \times \square = 27$

8. $6 \times \square = 48$ **16.** $81 \div 9 = \square$

▲▲▲

S P A C E

Draw a plan of your bedroom. Write the directions for going from the door to the bed. Include the number of steps.

_____

_____

_____

_____

_____

Write another set of directions for moving about in your bedroom. Get someone to check to see if they are correct.

_____

Draw the shapes you would get if you cut these cakes along the dotted lines.

1.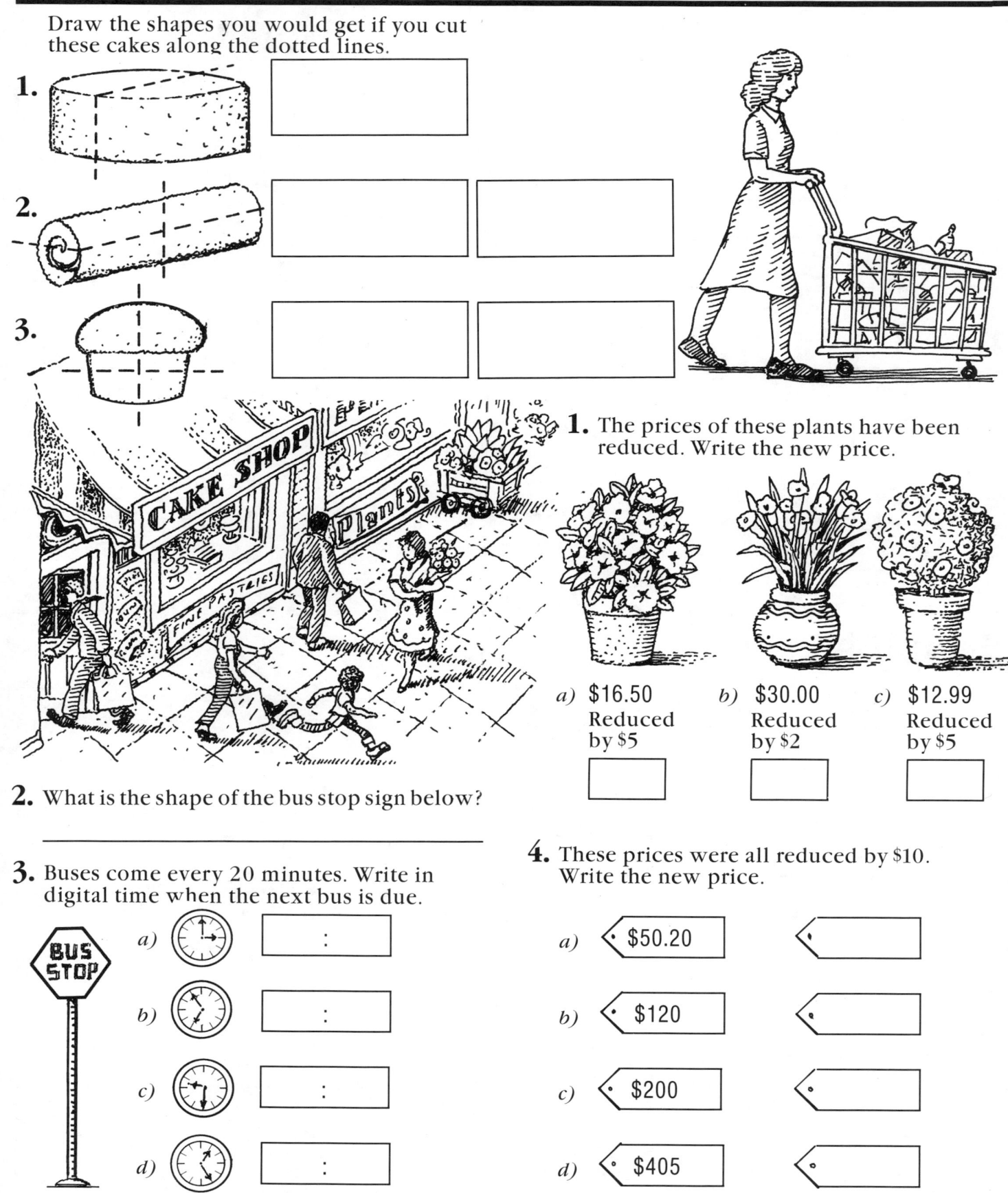

2.

3.

1. The prices of these plants have been reduced. Write the new price.

a) $16.50
Reduced by $5

b) $30.00
Reduced by $2

c) $12.99
Reduced by $5

2. What is the shape of the bus stop sign below?

_____

3. Buses come every 20 minutes. Write in digital time when the next bus is due.

a) [:   ]

b) [:   ]

c) [:   ]

d) [:   ]

4. These prices were all reduced by $10. Write the new price.

a) $50.20

b) $120

c) $200

d) $405

This graph shows shoppers going to the Hardware Shop one Saturday morning.

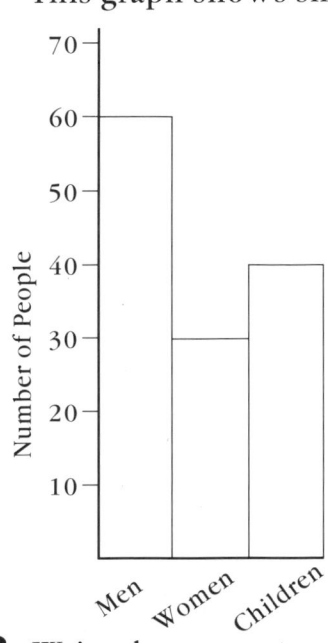

1. *a)* How many went through the shop doors on Saturday morning?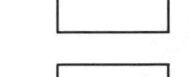

b) How many more men than children?

c) How many more men than women?

d) Half of the men purchased goods. How many was this?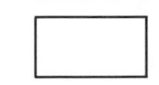

2. Write the amounts on the price tickets.

a) Eighty-six dollars and ninety cents

b) One hundred and fifty dollars and fifty cents

c) Six hundred and forty-nine dollars and fifty cents

d) Seven hundred and five dollars and ninety-five cents

3. *a)* 9  s cost

b) 7 s cost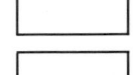

c) 5  s cost

d) 10 s cost

e) If I bought 3  s, what change would I get back from $20?

f) What would be the total cost of 5 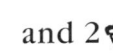 , 2 and 2  ?

4. These items are half price. What would they cost?

a)  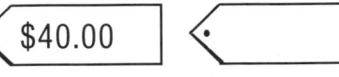 $40.00

b) $26.00

c) $90.00

5. These packets have bulbs in them. How many bulbs altogether?

a)_____ b)_____ c)_____

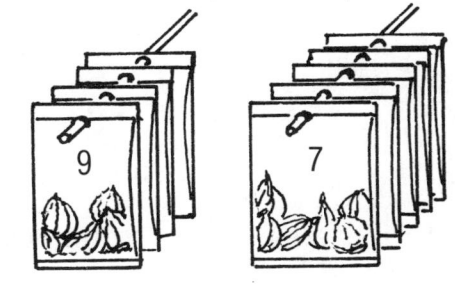
8   9   7

NUMBER

Using  show 8.0 on your calculator. Add a number to make 8.7.

What did you add? ☐

Try these:

Key in	Add	To make
7.0		7.6
3.00		3.47
2.0		2.9
6.00		6.43

1. 8 x 4 = ☐
2. 8 x 6 = ☐
3. 1 x 8 = ☐
4. 5 x 8 = ☐
5. 8 x 3 = ☐
6. 2 x 8 = ☐
7. 8 x 7 = ☐
8. 10 x 8 = ☐
9. 8 x 8 = ☐
10. 8 x 9 = ☐
11. ☐ x 8 = 64
12. ☐ x 8 = 56
13. 8 x ☐ = 72
14. 8 x ☐ = 48

1. 40 – 6 = ☐
2. 63 – 7 = ☐
3. 95 – 7 = ☐
4. 35 – 6 = ☐
5. 61 – 6 = ☐
6. 82 – 7 = ☐
7. 83 – 6 = ☐
8. 46 – 7 = ☐
9. 22 – 6 = ☐
10. 60 – 7 = ☐
11. 54 – 6 = ☐
12. 70 – 7 = ☐
13. 74 – 7 = ☐
14. 46 – 6 = ☐

MEASUREMENT

You'll need a square centimetre grid or Centicubes. Find these objects and estimate then measure the number of square centimetres needed to cover the surface.

Object	Estimate	Measurement	Difference
ERASER			
✉			
BUTTER			
(ruler)			

How many square centimetres in the sole of this shoe? ☐

How many square centimetres is the sole of your shoe? ☐

⊔ = 1 cm

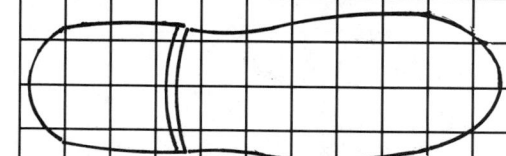

This array shows 3 x 8. 3 and 8 are factors of 24.

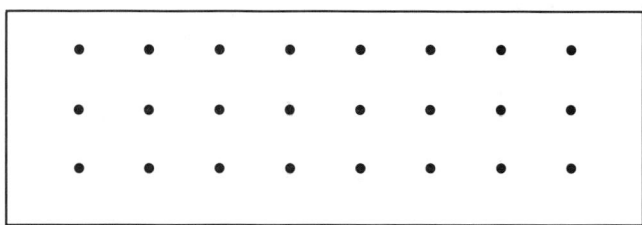

Make two arrays for 24 to show other factors of 24.

1. ☐ 1 x 1 or 1 squared   = ☐

2. ☐☐ 2 x 2 or 2 squared = ☐
☐☐

3. ☐☐☐
☐☐☐ 3 x 3 or   = ☐
☐☐☐ 3 squared

1. 4 x 2 = 8, 4 and 2 are factors of ☐.

2. 2, 6, 3 and 4 are factors of ☐.

3. Factors of 36 are ☐.

4. Factors of 18 are ☐.

S P A C E

Colour each of these shapes a different colour.

The shapes have now been broken into 2. Put them back together by colouring the matching pieces.

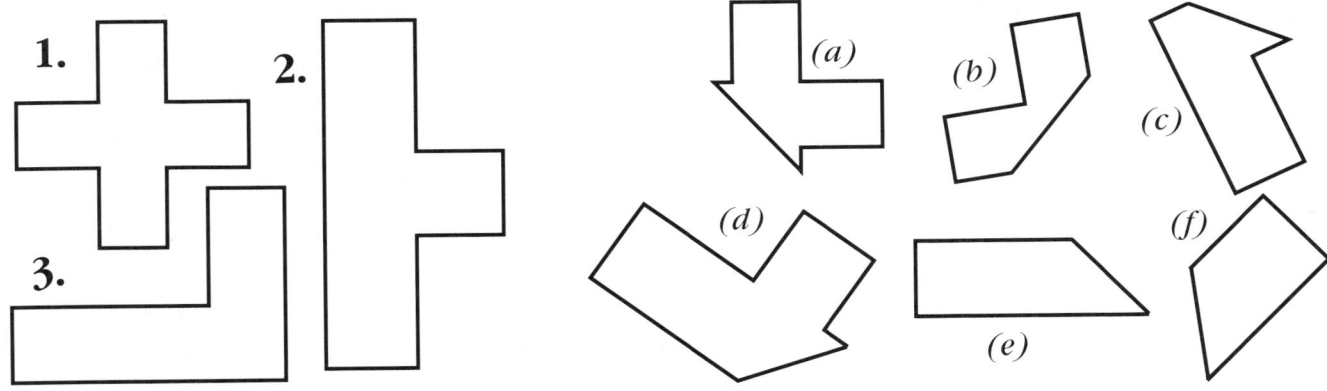

1.

2.

3.

(a)
(b)
(c)
(d)
(e)
(f)

Sketch the shapes you would get if you cut these shapes along the broken lines.

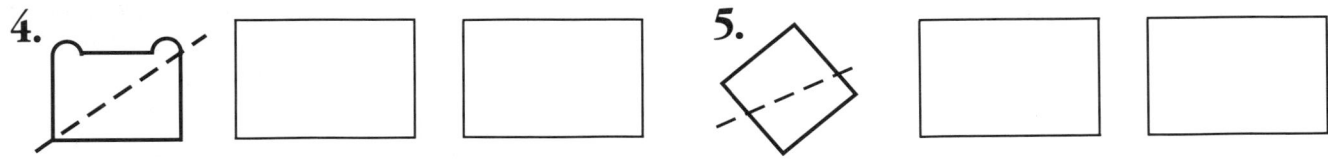

4.

5.

NUMBER

The cost of the mystery parcels is shown.
Draw the dollar notes you could use to buy them.

1. $65

2. $125

3. $235

4. $115

1.	7 x 4 = ☐	1. 52 ÷ 8 = ☐
2.	7 x 7 = ☐	2. 71 ÷ 9 = ☐
3.	5 x 7 = ☐	3. 8 ÷ 64 = ☐
4.	7 x 2 = ☐	4. 33 ÷ 9 = ☐
5.	9 x 7 = ☐	5. 55 ÷ 9 = ☐
6.	3 x 7 = ☐	6. 8 ÷ 83 = ☐
7.	7 x 1 = ☐	7. 9 ÷ 27 = ☐
8.	7 x 6 = ☐	8. 65 ÷ 8 = ☐
9.	7 x 8 = ☐	9. 84 ÷ 9 = ☐
10.	10 x 7 = ☐	10. 27 ÷ 8 = ☐
11.	7 x ☐ = 49	11. 46 ÷ 9 = ☐
12.	☐ x 7 = 35	12. 58 ÷ 9 = ☐
13.	7 x ☐ = 56	13. 78 ÷ 8 = ☐
14.	☐ x 7 = 42	14. 36 ÷ 8 = ☐
15.	7 x ☐ = 63	15. 42 ÷ 9 = ☐
16.	☐ x 7 = 28	16. 49 ÷ 8 = ☐

MEASUREMENT

1. Draw lines to match these times.

(a) 20 past 5 in the morning   12.06 p.m.
(b) 1 o'clock in the afternoon   5.00 p.m.
(c) 5 o'clock in the afternoon   1.00 a.m.
(d) 3 o'clock in the morning   1.00 p.m.
(e) 6 minutes past 12 in the afternoon   5.20 a.m.
(f) 1 o'clock in the morning   3.00 a.m.

2. Order these times from earliest to latest.

6.20 a.m.   5.35 a.m.   5.25 p.m.   6.00 p.m.   8.00 a.m.

_____   _____   _____   _____   _____

3. Add 1 hour to:

(a) 11.15 a.m. _____
(b) 6.05 p.m. _____
(c) 11.52 p.m. _____

4. Are these morning or afternoon?

(a) 3.20 p.m. _____
(b) 9.30 a.m. _____
(c) 4.15 p.m. _____

5. Write the times shown to the nearest 5 minutes in digital time a.m./p.m.

(a)

(b)

(c)

1. Draw a 4 square.

4 squared =

2. Draw a 5 square.

5 squared =

3. Draw a 6 square.

6 squared =

4. Count on by nines.
You are writing multiples of 9.

9 —— —— —— —— ——

—— —— —— —— ——

5. Which number is not a multiple of 4?
4, 8, 16, 12, 15, 20, 24

6. Which number is not a multiple of 3?
3, 6, 9, 12, 15, 18, 21, 24, 25

Factor Quiz

7. My factors include 2, 3, 4, 6.
What number am I?

8. I am a multiple of 6.
My factors include 4 and 9.
What number am I?

9. I am a multiple of 2.
My factors include 3, 6, 9.
What number am I?

SPACE

In this shape you cannot see the face of every cube.

Write the number of cubes that have:

1 face visible _____

2 faces visible _____

3 faces visible _____

Draw the shape you would see if you looked at:

The top view of a saucepan.

The bottom view of a chair.

The side view of a hat.

UNIT 23

▲▲▲▲▲▲

NUMBER

1. On Monday 6 children forgot their homework. On Tuesday twice as many children forgot.
How many forgot on Tuesday?

2. The recipe needs 1 cup of flour to make enough for three people. If you want to make enough for three times as many people how much flour will be needed?

3. Sam has twice as many marbles as Jenny. Jenny has 9.
How many has Sam?

4. Arthur jogged 10 km last week. This week he wants to jog twice that far.
How far will he jog?

1. 7 x 0 = ☐
2. 7 x 5 = ☐
3. 3 x 7 = ☐
4. 6 x 7 = ☐
5. 7 x 1 = ☐
6. 10 x 7 = ☐
7. 7 x 7 = ☐
8. 7 x 2 = ☐
9. 7 x 8 = ☐
10. 7 x 9 = ☐
11. 4 x 7 = ☐
12. ☐ x 7 = 14
13. 7 x ☐ = 77
14. 7 x ☐ = 42
15. ☐ x 7 = 28
16. 7 x ☐ = 49
17. 7 x ☐ = 56

1. 42 – 8 = ☐
2. 38 – 9 = ☐
3. 63 – 8 = ☐
4. 44 – 8 = ☐
5. 86 – 9 = ☐
6. 53 – 9 = ☐
7. 75 – 8 = ☐
8. 42 – 9 = ☐
9. 61 – 9 = ☐
10. 86 – 8 = ☐
11. 74 – 9 = ☐
12. 91 – 8 = ☐
13. 30 – 8 = ☐
14. 25 – 9 = ☐
15. 47 – 9 = ☐
16. 32 – 8 = ☐
17. 80 – 9 = ☐

▲▲

MEASUREMENT

John measured items in his kitchen in metres and tenths of metres.

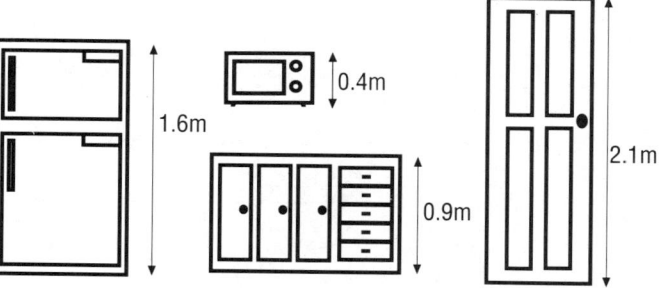

1.6m   0.4m   0.9m   2.1m

1. Is the height of the door closer to 2 m or 3 m?

2. Is the height of the fridge closer to 1 m or 2 m?

3. What is the difference between the height of the cupboards and the height of the fridge?

4. Round the height of the cupboards to the nearest metre.

5. If the microwave were put on top of the cupboard, how high would it reach?

6. Measure items in your kitchen in metres and tenths of metres:

kitchen door height	cupboard height	fridge height

1. 57 plus 26 = [   ]

2. Add 45 to 66 = [   ]

3. Double 39 = [   ]

4. To 15 add 69 = [   ]

5. 32 + 48 = [   ]

6. Total of 57 and 28 = [   ]

7. 46 and 39 = [   ]

8. 77 plus 16 = [   ]

Round off these numbers to the nearest thousand.

1. 6800 _____

2. 3150 _____

3. 4799 _____

4. 8204 _____

▲▲

S P A C E

Use these dots to make a maze of your own.

. . . .
. . . .
. . . .
. . . .
. . . .
. . . .
. . . .
. . . .
. . . .
. . . .

Draw these coloured shapes in the correct box.

Yellow ◯

Pink ▢

Pink △

Green ◯

	Yellow	Pink	Green
 △			
 ◯			
▢			

UNIT 24
▲▲▲▲▲▲

NUMBER

1. Draw lines to match the amounts with decimals.

    (a) 4250 mL   1.36m

    (b) 136 cm   8.42 m

    (c) 1 whole and 47 hundredths   4.25 L

    (d) 8 m 42 cm   0.6

    (e) 550 cm   1.47

    (f) 6 tenths   2.08 L

    (g) 2 litres and 80 mL   5.5 m

2. Complete this chart.

1 m 37 cm	8 m 20 cm	320 cm	1050 mL
1·37 m	m	m	L

1. 6 x 8 = ☐	1. 35 + 9 = ☐
2. 36 ÷ 6 = ☐	2. 86 + 7 = ☐
3. 10 x 6 = ☐	3. 39 + 6 = ☐
4. 6 x 3 = ☐	4. 79 + 8 = ☐
5. 48 ÷ 6 = ☐	5. 88 + 6 = ☐
6. 18 ÷ 6 = ☐	6. 56 + 9 = ☐
7. 6 x 9 = ☐	7. 28 + 8 = ☐
8. 54 ÷ 6 = ☐	8. 47 + 7 = ☐
9. 7 x 6 = ☐	9. 87 + 9 = ☐
10. 24 ÷ ☐ = 4	10. 27 + 6 = ☐
11. 6 x ☐ = 36	11. 57 + 8 = ☐
12. 42 ÷ 6 = ☐	12. 68 + 7 = ☐
13. 6 x 5 = ☐	13. 88 + 9 = ☐
14. 30 ÷ ☐ = 5	14. 56 + 6 = ☐
15. 6 x 4 = ☐	15. 49 + 9 = ☐

▲▲▲

MEASUREMENT

How many:

☐ 500g   to make   ☐ 1kg   ? _____

☐ 200g   to make   ☐ 1kg   ? _____

☐ 100g   to make   ☐ 1kg   ? _____

Look at the mass pieces on each balance. What is the mass of each object?

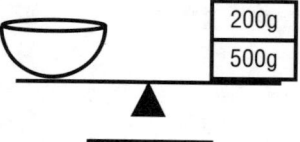
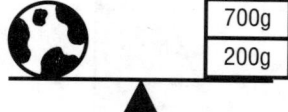
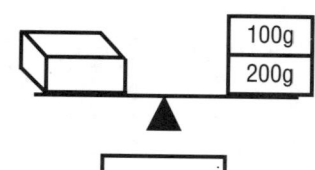

The total mass of the 3 objects is _____

Is the total mass more or less than 1 kg? _____ By how much? _____

1. 26 subtract 8 = ☐

2. I had 40 marbles, but lost 6. How many left? ☐

3. There were 50 sheep, then 37 died. How many left? ☐

4. There are 51 children on a bus; 28 are girls. How many are boys? ☐

5. There are 65 hens, 47 laid eggs. How many did not lay eggs? ☐

6. 72 pies were made. 16 were left in the shop. How many sold? ☐

What goes up but never comes down? To find the answer, work out the totals, then match the total with the letter below.

1. 33 + 22 = ☐

2. 49 + 16 = ☐

3. 18 + 18 = ☐

4. 19 + 32 = ☐

5. 16 + 16 = ☐

6. 14 + 23 = ☐

7. 2 + 9 + 6 = ☐

17	32	36	37	51	55	65
E	A	U	G	R	Y	O

___ ___ ___   ___ ___ ___ ___

SPACE

	Top View	Side View

Top View   Side View

Top View   Side View

Top View   Side View

Make these models then work out how many faces of each small cube you can see on each model.

		Sides Visible			
		3	2	1	0

1. Write directions for finding the treasure hidden in Danger Cave. Follow the route starting at Sandy Bay.

_____

_____

_____

_____

_____

_____

_____

2. The pirates travelled on the ship _Treasure Trove_. Write this information about its size in metres.

(a) Length   15 m 90 cm ☐

(b) Width   4 m 85 cm ☐

(c) Height of mast   550 cm ☐

(d) Length of cannon 120 cm ☐

3. The pirates were greedy. They wanted everything! Circle the largest number of jewels from the treasure chest.

(a) Diamonds   (b) Emeralds

8404   6929
8400   6930
8049   6999

(c) Rubies   4700
4790   4099

4. Every pirate received the following money from the treasure chest.
How much money in each pile?

(a) $5   (b) $100   (c) $50   (d) $10

    9   7   6   9

☐   ☐   ☐   ☐

(e) Use a calculator to work out how much money each pirate got. ☐

5. If the ship set sail on 25 June and the trip took 12 days, what date did the pirates arrive at Mystery Island? ☐

6. The pirates spent 5 days finding the treasure and taking it back to the ship. The sea trip back took 15 days because of a storm. What date did they arrive back? ☐

Solve the code to find the pirate's name.
Match the answer with the letter below.

9	8	6	8	6	60	6
x4	x3	x9	x8	x4	−7	x7

7	40	16	8	48	36	6	8
x8	−4	+8	x6	−9	−12	x6	x4

A	C	E	F	I	N	P	R	S	T
24	36	32	39	53	42	54	48	56	64

_____

_____

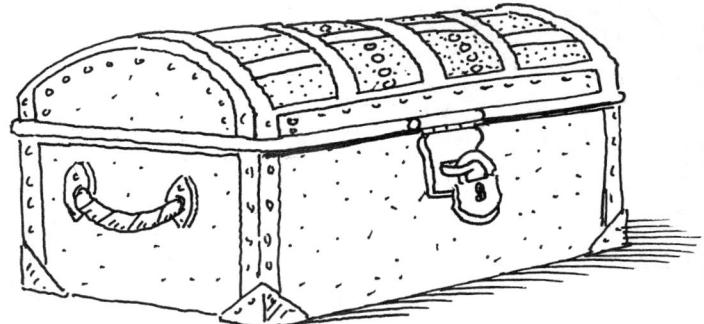

Draw the top of the chest. Then colour the pattern.

[blank box]

Solve these number problems.

1. There were 72 gold bars to be divided among 9 pirates. How many gold bars did each pirate receive? [ ]

2. There were 9 cannons on each side of the ship and 9 cannon balls for each cannon. How many cannon balls altogether? [ ]

3. If a crew member started his shift at 8.00 a.m. and came off at 5.30 p.m. how many hours was this? [ ]

4. If the ship's cook used two tins of meat each day that the pirates were at sea and three tins while on the island, how many were used altogether? [ ]

Design your own pirate flag.

Make it symmetrical on either side of the broken line.

[blank box with dashed vertical line]

UNIT 26

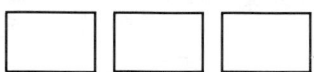

1. 2 and 4 are two factors of ⬜ and ⬜ .

2. The three smallest multiples of 8 are
⬜ ⬜ ⬜

3. What are the factors of 30?
⬜ .

4. The product of 3 and 6 is ⬜ .

5. What are the factors of 48?
⬜

6. List the multiples of 6 less than 30. ⬜

7. 16 is a multiple of ⬜ ⬜ ⬜ .

8. Which number does not belong? ⬜
8, 16, 25, 32, 40
Why? _____

9. The product of 6 and 8 is ⬜ .

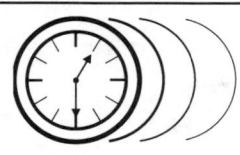

1. 9 x ⬜ = 18   1. 30 – 8 = ⬜
2. 9 ÷ 9 = ⬜   2. 51 – 6 = ⬜
3. 6 x ⬜ = 54   3. 82 – 7 = ⬜
4. 72 ÷ 9 = ⬜   4. 70 – 9 = ⬜
5. 9 x ⬜ = 9   5. 54 – 7 = ⬜
6. 36 ÷ ⬜ = 4   6. 72 – 6 = ⬜
7. 4 x 9 = ⬜   7. 51 – 8 = ⬜
8. 81 ÷ 9 = ⬜   8. 93 – 9 = ⬜
9. 9 x 6 = ⬜   9. 73 – 8 = ⬜
10. 63 ÷ 9 = ⬜   10. 94 – 6 = ⬜
11. ⬜ x 9 = 45   11. 21 – 7 = ⬜
12. ⬜ ÷ 9 = 7   12. 72 – 9 = ⬜
13. 9 x 9 = ⬜   13. 44 – 9 = ⬜
14. ⬜ ÷ 9 = 6   14. 62 – 8 = ⬜
15. 9 x ⬜ = 72   15. 43 – 7 = ⬜
16. 45 ÷ 9 = ⬜   16. 83 – 6 = ⬜
17. 9 x ⬜ = 63   17. 51 – 9 = ⬜
18. 27 ÷ 9 = ⬜   18. 84 – 8 = ⬜

---

1. Use a medicine glass to measure how many millilitres in these containers.

Container	Estimate	Measured Capacity
teaspoon		
egg cup		
dessert spoon		
drinking cup		

2. Circle the more likely capacity of these objects.

250 L
or
250 mL

400 mL
or
40 L

5 mL
or
5 L

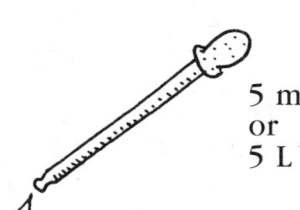
20 L
or
200 mL

---

1. 3 squared is _____ .

2. 4 squared is _____ .

3. 5 squared is _____ .

4. 6 squared is _____ .

5. 7 squared is _____ .

6. Draw squares of 6.

7. Draw squares of 7.

1. Write the numbers.

(a) 13 hundreds _____

(b) 2600 ones _____

(c) 700 tens _____

(d) 78 hundreds _____

(e) 4 thousands _____

2. Write these numbers in words.

(a) 4300 _____
_____

(b) 5060 _____
_____

Work out these.

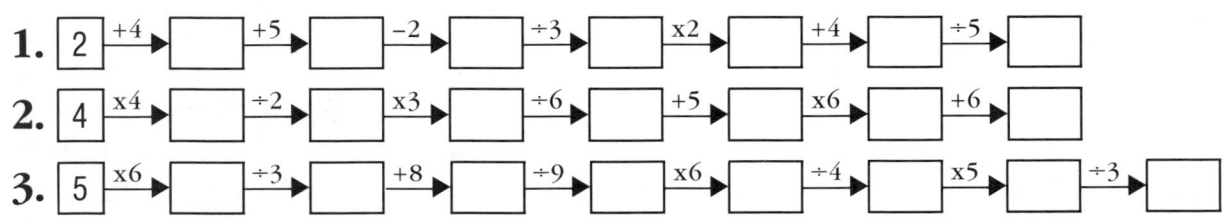

1. 2 → +4 → ☐ → +5 → ☐ → −2 → ☐ → ÷3 → ☐ → x2 → ☐ → +4 → ☐ → ÷5 → ☐

2. 4 → x4 → ☐ → ÷2 → ☐ → x3 → ☐ → ÷6 → ☐ → +5 → ☐ → x6 → ☐ → +6 → ☐

3. 5 → x6 → ☐ → ÷3 → ☐ → +8 → ☐ → ÷9 → ☐ → x6 → ☐ → ÷4 → ☐ → x5 → ☐ → ÷3 → ☐

S P A C E

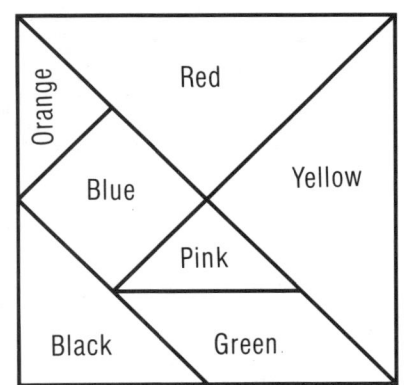

3. Colour the shapes the correct colours. Then draw and colour the missing shape.

1. Colour the shapes the correct colours.

2. Now find the shapes in the tangrams and colour them the same.

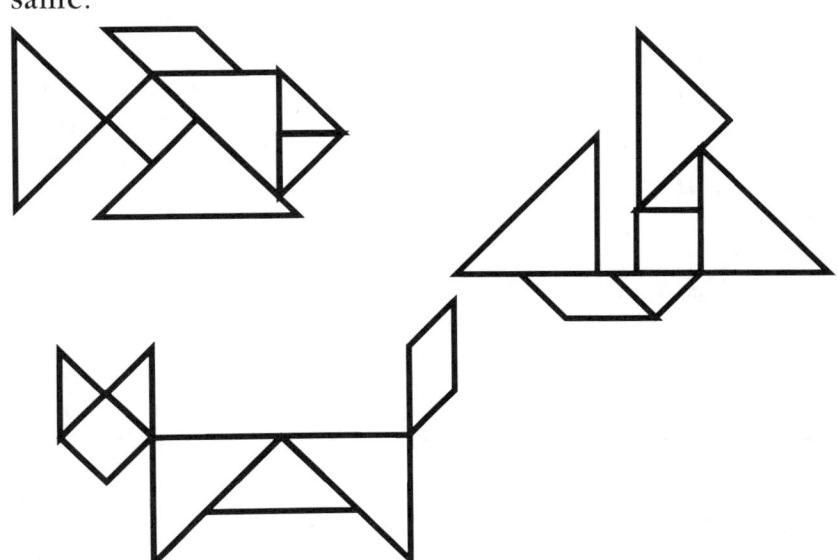

UNIT 27

NUMBER

1. There are 25 dog biscuits, and 3 dogs.

How many biscuits
for each dog?

How many left over?

2. There are 25 cat treats, and 4 cats.

How many treats
for each cat?

How many left over?

3. There are 17 canaries, and 3 cages.

How many canaries
to each cage?

How many left over?

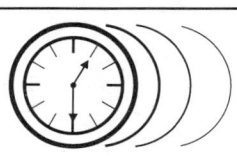

1. $\square \times 8 = 32$ 1. $9 \times 2 = \square$
2. $64 \div 8 = \square$ 2. $7 \times 7 = \square$
3. $9 \times \square = 72$ 3. $5 \times 9 = \square$
4. $48 \div 8 = \square$ 4. $8 \times 9 = \square$
5. $5 \times 8 = \square$ 5. $6 \times 9 = \square$
6. $56 \div 8 = \square$ 6. $7 \times 6 = \square$
7. $\square \times 8 = 56$ 7. $5 \times 8 = \square$
8. $72 \div 8 = \square$ 8. $7 \times 9 = \square$
9. $6 \times \square = 48$ 9. $5 \times 7 = \square$
10. $8 \times 8 = \square$ 10. $4 \times 9 = \square$
11. $64 \div 8 = \square$ 11. $8 \times 8 = \square$
12. $32 \div 8 = \square$ 12. $4 \times 8 = \square$
13. $\square \times 8 = 24$ 13. $5 \times 6 = \square$
14. $24 \div \square = 3$ 14. $7 \times 8 = \square$
15. $\square \times 8 = 56$ 15. $6 \times 6 = \square$

MEASUREMENT

John and Lee made scales for their
thermometers.

John

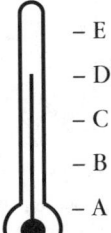

– E
– D
– C
– B
– A

Lee

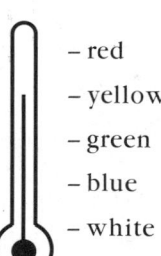

– red
– yellow
– green
– blue
– white

1. What temperature is on
Lee's scale?

2. What is the temperature
on John's scale?

3. If the temperature is white
on Lee's scale what would
it be on John's?

4. If the temperature is C on John's
scale what would it be on Lee's?

5. What temperature would be
very hot:
on Lee's scale?

on John's?

6. What temperature would be
very cold:
on Lee's scale?

on John's?

7. Which temperature scale
do you prefer?

Why?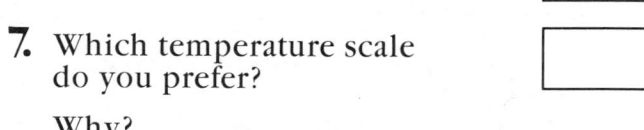

Try this Addition Crossnumber Puzzle.

Across
1. Number before 900
3. Number after 410
5. 300 + 300
6. 5 x 6
7. 500 – 9
8. 90 – 42
9. Half of 164
10. 4649 + 1
11. 6 x 7
12. 9000 + 800
13. 6 + 8 + 7 + 9 + 7

Down
1. 68 + 19
2. Number after 9000
3. 5 x 9
4. 10 x 10
5. Double 346
6. 400 – 15
7. 4 x 12
8. 92 ÷ 2
10. 410 + 10
11. 8 x 5

1. 6000 and one more thousand ▢

2. One more hundred than 6700 ▢

3. One thousand less than 8000 ▢

4. 10 more than 3690 ▢

5. 100 less than 7000 ▢

1. 9 x 9 = ▢

2. 6 x 8 = ▢

3. 7 x 6 = ▢

4. 9 x 4 = ▢

5. 6 x 6 = ▢

6. 7 x 8 = ▢

7. 9 x 6 = ▢

8. 8 x 9 = ▢

9. 9 x 5 = ▢

▲▲

S P A C E

You will need A4-size paper for these activities.

Rectangular piece of paper

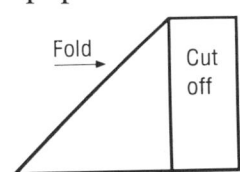
Fold → Cut off

Fold corner across

Cut off the shaded parts

Draw the shape you get when you open the paper. ▭

Draw the shape here. ▭

It is called a __ __ __ __ __ __ __ .

Take a circular piece of paper.

Fold it in half.

Open it and fold it again.

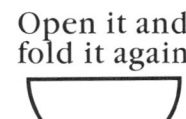
Fold in Fold in
Fold in Fold in

You have made a

_____

UNIT 28
▲▲▲▲▲▲

These division problems have a remainder.

1. 49 ÷ 8 = ☐ r ☐

2. 36 ÷ 5 = ☐ r ☐

3. 41 ÷ 8 = ☐ r ☐

4. 26 ÷ 4 = ☐ r ☐

5. 45 ÷ 10 = ☐ r ☐

6. 66 ÷ 10 = ☐ r ☐

7. $\overset{10\ r\ 2}{4\overline{)\ \square\ \square}}$

8. $\overset{11\ r\ 3}{6\overline{)\ \square\ \square}}$

9. $\overset{21\ r\ 1}{3\overline{)\ \square\ \square}}$

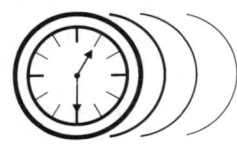

1. 49 ÷ 7 = ☐	1. 7 x 9 = ☐
2. 7 x 9 = ☐	2. 8 x 8 = ☐
3. ☐ x 7 = 14	3. 9 x 9 = ☐
4. 42 ÷ ☐ = 6	4. 8 x 6 = ☐
5. ☐ x 7 = 42	5. 6 x 9 = ☐
6. 35 ÷ 7 = ☐	6. 7 x 8 = ☐
7. 7 x ☐ = 56	7. 5 x 8 = ☐
8. 3 x 7 = ☐	8. 8 x 9 = ☐
9. 56 ÷ ☐ = 8	9. 6 x 6 = ☐
10. 28 ÷ 7 = ☐	10. 7 x 7 = ☐
11. 7 x 7 = ☐	11. 5 x 9 = ☐
12. ☐ ÷ 7 = 3	12. 6 x 5 = ☐
13. 4 x 7 = ☐	13. 7 x 6 = ☐
14. ☐ ÷ 7 = 9	14. 9 x 6 = ☐
15. 7 x ☐ = 35	15. 4 x 7 = ☐
16. 70 ÷ 7 = ☐	16. 9 x 8 = ☐

Write these decimals in words.

1. 1·9 _____

2. 0·6 _____

3. 3·71 _____

4. 0·38 _____

5. 6·06 _____

What are the areas of these shapes in square centimetres?

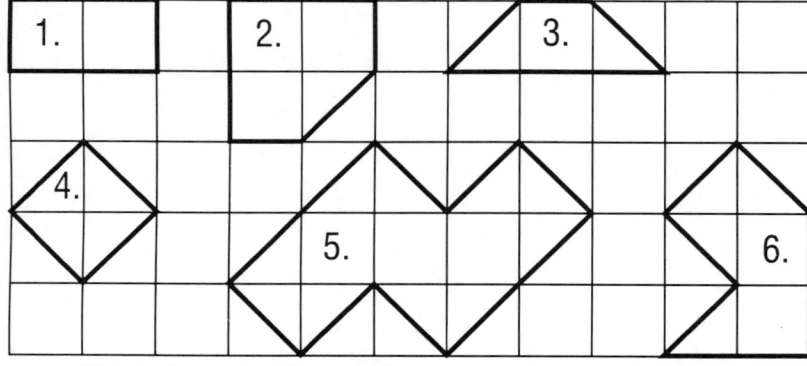

1. _____ cm²   **4.** _____ cm²

2. _____ cm²   **5.** _____ cm²

3. _____ cm²   **6.** _____ cm²

Find the area (in cm²) and perimeter (in cm) of these shapes.

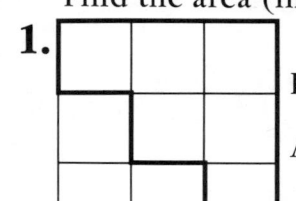

1. Perimeter = _____ cm

Area = _____ cm²

2. Perimeter = _____ cm

Area = _____ cm²

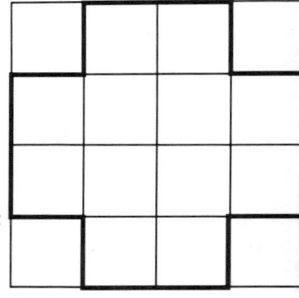

Which is larger?

1. 0·9 or 0·16 [ ]

2. 0·8 or 0·89 [ ]

3. 0·34 or 0·43 [ ]

4. 1·3 or 1·03 [ ]

5. 1·0 or 0·99 [ ]

Have	Spend	Change
1. $5	$3	[ ]
2. $5	$1.50	[ ]
3. $5	80c	[ ]
4. $5	$4.50	[ ]
5. $5	$0.10	[ ]

There are 15 errors in this multiplication table.
Can you find them? Colour in the squares where the errors are.

X	1	2	3	4	5	6	7	8	9	10
1	1	2	3	4	0	6	7	8	9	10
2	2	3	6	9	10	12	14	17	18	20
3	3	6	9	12	15	19	21	24	27	30
4	0	8	12	16	22	24	28	32	36	40
5	5	10	15	20	25	30	36	40	45	55
6	6	12	18	24	36	36	42	48	54	60
7	7	14	20	28	35	42	49	54	63	70
8	8	16	24	32	40	48	56	64	72	80
9	9	18	27	36	46	54	63	72	82	90
10	10	22	30	40	50	60	70	80	90	100

SPACE

1. Colour the boxes.

   (a) Green – Bottom shelf third from right

   (b) Red – Top shelf second from left

   (c) Blue – Bottom shelf first from right

2. What is the position of boxes marked:

   (a) [▨] ? _____

   (b) [⦂⦂] ? _____

UNIT 29

▲▲▲▲▲▲

1.

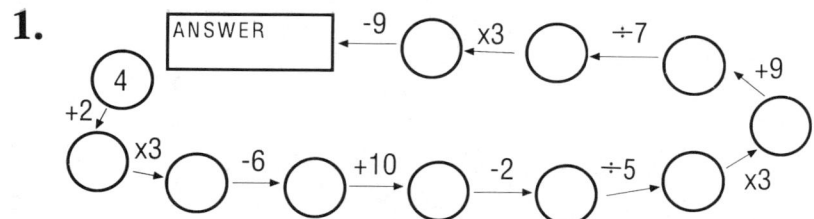

2.

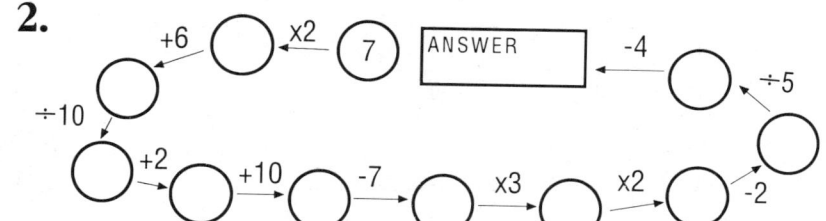

3.

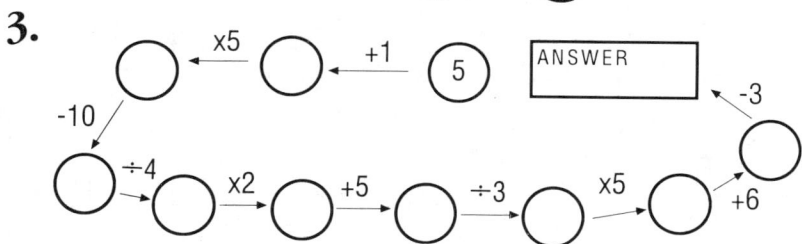

1. ☐ x 8 = 64	1. 6 + 4 = ☐
2. 4 x ☐ = 36	2. 8 + 3 = ☐
3. ☐ x 9 = 0	3. 9 + 7 = ☐
4. 9 x ☐ = 90	4. 6 + 2 = ☐
5. 7 x ☐ = 49	5. 4 + 0 = ☐
6. ☐ x 3 = 27	6. 1 + 9 = ☐
7. 9 x ☐ = 81	7. 2 + 7 = ☐
8. ☐ x 6 = 36	8. 3 + 7 = ☐
9. ☐ x 8 = 32	9. 7 + 5 = ☐
10. 7 x ☐ = 42	10. 5 + 8 = ☐
11. ☐ x 6 = 30	11. 7 + 8 = ☐
12. 9 x ☐ = 72	12. 3 + 9 = ☐
13. ☐ x 8 = 48	13. 5 + 2 = ☐
14. 4 x ☐ = 28	14. 2 + 6 = ☐
15. 6 x ☐ = 6	15. 4 + 6 = ☐
16. 8 x ☐ = 56	16. 1 + 7 = ☐

▲▲▲

M E A S U R E M E N T

Do you remember the twelve months, in order?

Month	Number of Days

Days of week	How many?
	_____ secs in 1 min
	_____ mins in 1 hr
	_____ hrs in 1 day
	_____ days in 1 week
	_____ weeks in a fortnight
	_____ decades in a century
	_____ years in a century

Order from smallest to largest: day, second, week, decade, hour, century, minute, fortnight. _____

_____

How many days until the end of the school year? _____

How many days until the end of the year? _____

CALCULATOR TARGETS

1. You can only press these keys:

 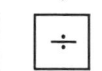

(a) Make your display read 7.
Write what you did.

_____

_____

_____

(b) Make your display read 13.
How did you do it?

_____

_____

_____

2. You can only press these keys:

(a) Make your display read 17.
Write what you did.

_____

_____

_____

(b) How many keystrokes did you use? ____

(c) Can you do it a different way? _____

_____

_____

S P A C E

1. Use geostrips and paper fasteners to make the shapes below. Try pushing each shape to make a new shape. Draw the new shapes you make.

(a)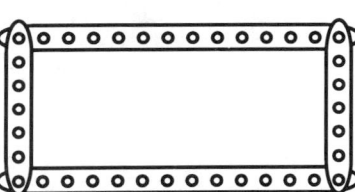

(b)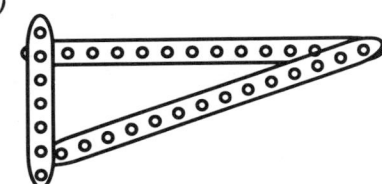

(c)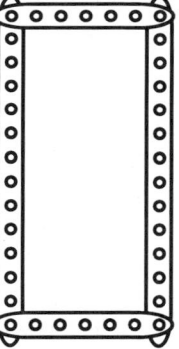

2. *(a)* Which shapes are non-rigid? _____

(b) Draw what you would do to make the shapes rigid.

Let's Go On A Vacation

HOLIDAY AT THE BEACH

Overnight Accommodation
   Double Room $98
   Single Room $65

....

Car Hire
   Daily Rate $55

1. How much would it cost to hire a car for 2 days and have a double room for 3 nights?

2. What is the difference in price between a double and single room?

3. Write these amounts in numbers. They are holiday costs.
   a) Four thousand two hundred and six dollars.
   b) Four thousand six hundred and twenty dollars.
   c) Four thousand six hundred and six dollars.

4. Work out the flying time:
   a) Sydney – Gold Coast
   b) Sydney – Brisbane
   c) Sydney – Rockhampton
   d) Sydney – Cairns

SYDNEY AIRPORT		
Destination	Departure Time	Arrival Time
Gold Coast	1.15	2.10
Brisbane	1.30	2.35
Rockhampton	2.10	3.45
Cairns	2.30	5.10

5. On the thermometer, colour to show the temperature it is likely to be outside:

   a) in the snow

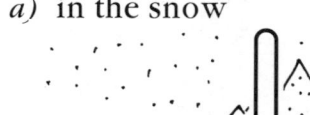

   b) at the beach in summer.

6. These fares will be reduced by $100 as part of a special Christmas offer. What will the new fare be?

$1960

$5199

$6000

$2099

THE PICNIC SET

ONLY
$55
a set

Individual Items

Mug $9

Plate $18

Knife $4

Fork $3

Spoon $2

Case $27

1.
a) How much would it cost to buy the items individually?

b) How much change would you have from $80?

c) What do you save by buying the set?

d) What would it cost to buy 2 sets of cutlery?

e) What change would you have from $20?

f) What would it cost to buy 2 mugs and 2 plates?

g) What change would you have from $60?

h) How much change would you get from $50 if you bought a full set without the case?

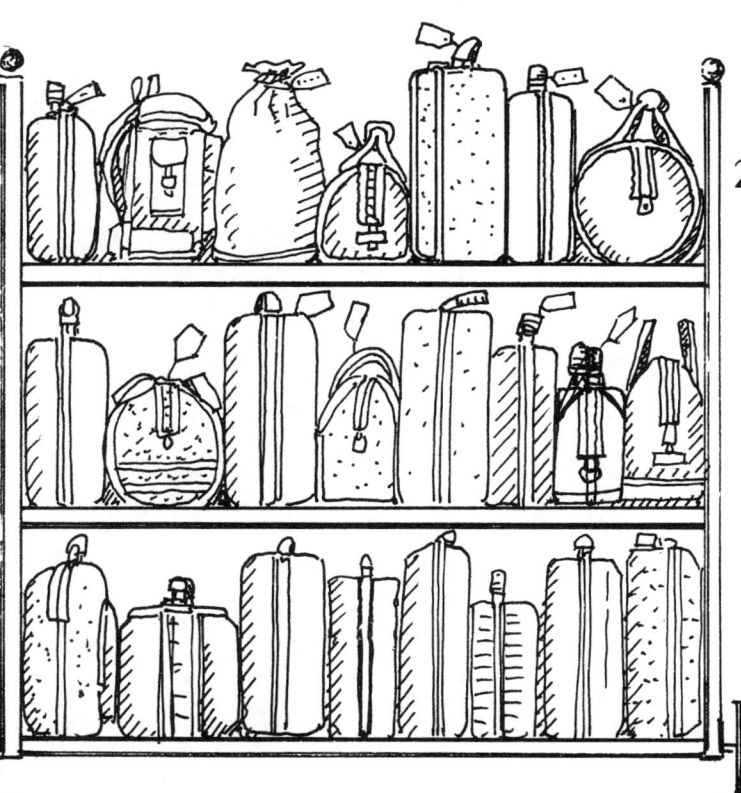

2. Locate and colour Sarah's luggage on the baggage trolley.

a) Her small red suitcase is on the bottom shelf fifth from the right.

b) Her overnight case is on the second shelf second from the right. It is blue.

c) Her large suitcase is black and is on the top shelf and third from the right.

3.
a) If the mass of Sarah's red suitcase was 28kg, the black suitcase 46kg and the overnight bag 13kg what was the total mass of her luggage?

b) If the first 78kg was carried free but every kg over that cost $4 a kg what would Sarah have to pay?

UNIT	Number	Measurement	Space	Write your own comments.
1	☐	☐	☐	_____
2	☐	☐	☐	_____
3	☐	☐	☐	_____
4	☐	☐	☐	_____
5	**The Zoo** _____			
6	☐	☐	☐	_____
7	☐	☐	☐	_____
8	☐	☐	☐	_____
9	☐	☐	☐	_____
10	**Fairytales** _____			
11	☐	☐	☐	_____
12	☐	☐	☐	_____
13	☐	☐	☐	_____
14	☐	☐	☐	_____
15	**The Circus** _____			
16	☐	☐	☐	_____
17	☐	☐	☐	_____
18	☐	☐	☐	_____
19	☐	☐	☐	_____
20	**At the Shopping Centre** _____			
21	☐	☐	☐	_____
22	☐	☐	☐	_____
23	☐	☐	☐	_____
24	☐	☐	☐	_____
25	**Pirates** _____			
26	☐	☐	☐	_____
27	☐	☐	☐	_____
28	☐	☐	☐	_____
29	☐	☐	☐	_____
30	**Let's Go On a Vacation** _____			